P9-DCM-815

CHICAGO
Food Crawls

Soo Park

TOURING *the* NEIGHBORHOODS
ONE BITE & LIBATION *at a* TIME

Globe
Pequot

GUILFORD, CONNECTICUT

Globe
Pequot

An imprint of The Rowman & Littlefield Publishing Group, Inc.
4501 Forbes Blvd., Ste. 200
Lanham, MD 20706
www.rowman.com

Distributed by NATIONAL BOOK NETWORK

British Library Cataloguing in Publication Information available

Library of Congress Cataloging-in-Publication Data available

ISBN 978-1-4930-3769-8 (paperback)
ISBN 978-1-4930-3770-4 (e-book)

∞™ The paper used in this publication meets the minimum requirements of American National Standard for Information Sciences—Permanence of Paper for Printed Library Materials, ANSI/NISO Z39.48-1992

Printed in the United States of America

*This book is affectionately dedicated to my husband, Ron,
who has always encouraged me to pursue my dreams and passions.
It is also lovingly dedicated to my beautiful daughter, Chloe,
who motivates me to turn my dreams and passions into reality.*

Contents

Introduction

CHICAGO IS RENOWNED FOR SO MANY MAGNIFICENT ATTRIBUTES— its rich history, loyal sports fans, world-class museums and art, designer shops, vibrant neighborhoods—but my personal Chicago favorite is, of course, the fabulous food. There was a time when Chicago food simply meant Chicago classics, like Italian beef sandwiches and "Chicago-style" deep-dish pizza, hot dogs, and popcorn, or perhaps everybody's favorite mom-and-pop neighborhood gem around the corner that's been open for decades. Yes, sign me up for all of that, but there is so much more. Chicago has become one of the top, if not *the* top, culinary destinations in the world, with new restaurants and food concepts opening seemingly every day. Join me as I eat my way through the city.

Whether you call Chicago home or are just passing through, and whether you call it The Chi, ChiTown, Windy City, Second City, City of Big Shoulders, or "My Kind of Town, Chicago is . . . " a culinary mecca and foodie's paradise. From Michelin-rated to James Beard award–winning to comfort-food to fine-dining establishments, this book has something for you. It was a tough gig, but I took one for the team and visited over 150 restaurants from Bridgeport to Evanston and from Lake Michigan to Logan Square to assemble delectable and gut-busting Chicago Food Crawls.

Our crawl through Chicago will start in the south and move north and west. In the book, I reference "The Loop," which is the heart of Downtown Chicago where the "L" train actually forms a loop; from here, all the train lines shoot off north, west, and south. Thank you for taking this food journey with me; I am very excited to share my take on Chicago's most fabulous restaurants.

Follow the Icons

 If you eat something outrageous and don't take a photo for Instagram, did you really eat it? These restaurants feature dishes that are Instagram famous. These foods must be seen (and snapped) to be believed, and luckily they taste as good as they look!

 Cheers to a fabulous night out in Chicago! These spots add a little glam to your grub and are perfect for marking a special occasion.

 Follow this icon when you're crawling for cocktails. This symbol points out the establishments that are best known for their great drinks. The food never fails here, but be sure to come thirsty, too!

 This icon means that sweet treats are ahead. Bring your sweet tooth to these spots for dessert first (or second or third).

Chicago is for brunch. Look for this icon when crawling with a crew that needs sweet and savory (or an excuse to drink before noon).

THE BRIDGEPORT CRAWL

1. But first, brunch at **NANA**, 3267 S. HALSTED ST., CHICAGO, (312) 929-2486, NANAORGANIC.COM

2. Drink all day at **MARIA'S PACKAGED GOODS & COMMUNITY BAR**, 960 W. 31ST ST., CHICAGO, (773) 890-0588, COMMUNITY-BAR.COM

3. Slam it up at **KIMSKI**, 954-960 W. 31ST ST., CHICAGO, (773) 823-7336, KIMSKICHICAGO.COM

4. Wake up early for **BRIDGEPORT BAKERY**, 2907 S. ARCHER AVE., CHICAGO, (772) 523-1121

5. Quack on over to **THE DUCK INN**, 2701 S. ELEANOR ST., CHICAGO, (312) 724-8811, THEDUCKINNCHICAGO.COM

6. Sugarcoat everything at **26TH STREET SUGAR SHACK**, 630 W. 26TH ST., CHICAGO, (312) 225-6568, SUGARSHACKON26TH.COM

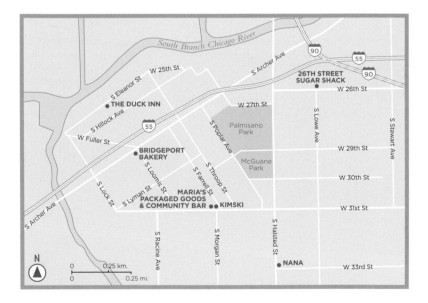

Bridgeport

Unity in Food Diversity

CHICAGO'S DIVERSITY IS ONE OF ITS GREATEST FEATURES, and there are few neighborhoods as diverse as Bridgeport. Often known as the first neighborhood in Chicago, Bridgeport is a working-class neighborhood located 3 short miles south of the Loop, just south of Pilsen and Chinatown, down by Guaranteed Rate Field—home of the Chicago White Sox. The area was first home to many Irish Americans who settled there while working on the Illinois and Michigan Canal, and since the mid-1800s it has also been home to Italian, German, Lithuanian, and Chinese Americans. Today, Bridgeport is still home to many of these cultures, along with a new focus on the arts as exemplified by the revitalized Bridgeport Art Center and Zhou B Art Center, which has helped bring attention and people to visit Bridgeport and its up-and-coming restaurant scene.

1

NANA

Ooh, Nana . . . what's your name? In 2009, brothers Omar and Christian Solis opened **NANA** (named after their mother, Maria "Nana" Solis) because of the lack of dining options in their neighborhood. The menu focuses on Latin-inspired dishes using organic, sustainable ingredients and attracts a loyal brunch crowd.

You can feel good about what you're eating because the ingredients are sourced from local purveyors, and they are free of preservatives, chemicals, toxins, food colorings, and pesticides. Everything is made in-house from scratch, including the cured meats, pickles, preserves, pastries, and breads.

The signature Nanadict is an obligatory order at brunch. Traditional Mexican *sopes,* also known as fried masa, are topped with chorizo, two poached eggs, and poblano cream and served with a side of greens and home fries. For sharing, try the Avocado Fries. It may sound a little odd, but it's oddly fantastic: Avocado wedges are covered in a seasoned batter and delicately fried, creating a harmonious crunchy and creamy balance. You will go nuts for the Peanut Butter Cocoa Pancakes with banana cream, walnuts, and whipped cream. If you are looking for a savory option, the Shrimp & Oyster Po'boy is calling your name. The combination of grilled shrimp and fried oyster adds a unique twist, while the house giardiniera and Cajun mayo gives it a little heat.

2 MARIA'S PACKAGED GOODS & COMMUNITY BAR

Part liquor store and part tavern, **MARIA'S PACKAGED GOODS & COMMUNITY BAR** is a chill, laid-back spot for daytime drinking, nighttime drinking, or all-day drinking . . . heck, it's 5 o'clock somewhere. South Korean native Maria Marszewski took over what was formerly known as Kaplan's Liquor in the 1980s. The neighborhood was not receptive to a new Asian, female proprietor. But through her warmth and kindness, she won the hearts of many and is still known as the community's maternal figure. Don't let her sweet demeanor fool you, though. She's tough, hardworking, and won't take any absurdity from anyone. I have nothing but mad respect for this lady.

Her two sons, Ed and Mike, took over the business in 2010 and transformed the divey bar into a hip hangout with a vast selection of craft beers, signature cocktails, and various whiskeys and spirits.

Get invigorated by the Corpse Reviver with gin, Cocchi Americano, Cointreau, lemon juice, and an absinthe rinse. The Palmer's Pint with house-infused ginger peach vodka, black tea, and organic lemonade is described on the menu as "a full pint of loveliness." Try a classic 11th Ward Old Fashioned with bourbon, a demerara sugar cube, bitters, and cherries. On their seasonal cocktail menu, you can find concoctions like the 210 Smith Street, with gin, egg white, lemon juice, and house grenadine. With drink in hand, head down the counter to Kimski.

KIMSKI

No need to crawl far for this next stop. **KIMSKI** is a counter-service extension of Maria's Packaged Goods & Community Bar and serves a mash-up of Korean-Polish street food creations by chef Won Kim, winner of the Food Network's *Cutthroat Kitchen*. The concept came about during KoPo BBQ nights hosted by the Marszewski brothers, when they served Polish sausages with kraut chi (sauerkraut kimchi) and other foods they grew up eating in the back patio of the bar.

Kim heavily researched the flavor profiles of the Polish and Korean cultures and mastered an informed balance of richness and acidity, paying homage to each side. He lightheartedly states that he's not here to impress any grandmothers, so don't expect 100 percent authentic Korean or Polish. He keeps it real.

As a Korean with many Polish friends, I've never thought of inter-mixing Korean and Polish cuisines, but it completely makes sense. There are a lot of similar flavor profiles between the two cultures, including Korean kimchi and Polish sauerkraut. and Korean *mandu* (dumplings) and Polish pierogies.

The Maria's Standard is what started it all. Their preopening video made by Daily Planet Productions tells the story the best. It starts off with two kids sitting at each end of the long dinner table: on one side is a European boy with a plate of Polish food and, on the other, an Asian girl with a plate of Korean food. The boy throws a Polish sausage across the table and inevitably starts a food fight. As they go back and forth, "slamming" each other with food, they create the ultimate fusion of two cultures, a Polish sausage with Korean kimchi, aka Maria's Standard. Google it. It's hilarious. Oh, and the soju mustard is a game-changer.

The Kopo Wangs are smoky, crispy, sweet, and spicy. You'll want to slather that sauce on everything. The Bing Bong Bowl is a bowl of comfort with five different kinds of rotating side vegetables over rice, topped with a fried egg and sweet-and-spicy sauce. Side dishes are made in-house using locally sourced ingredients. Cheese curds, anyone? The Kimski Poutine is doused with a flavorful kimchi gravy and topped with pickled onions, scallions, and sesame leaves; it's vegetarian-friendly, but meat can be added for an additional charge.

TIP

There is no lack of creativeness in Kimski's, so check the menu frequently. You'll see over-the-top offerings like the **Puff Daddy Burger**: organic grass-fed beef patty is padded between two pizza puffs. *Mind = blown*

4 BRIDGEPORT BAKERY

BRIDGEPORT BAKERY is a long-standing, no-frills bakery highly sought for their bacon buns, pączkis, cakes, doughnuts, and cookies. Even with their minimal online presence and little-to-no marketing efforts, droves of people still visit the bakery every day. Get there bright and early because treats fly off the shelves fast. Great news for all you morning people: They open at 5 a.m.

You won't find any trendy, Instagrammable, rainbow-colored, $10 treats here; instead you'll get simple, old-school, scrumptious, affordable treats. It is so inexpensive that I thought they made a mistake on my receipt. I wish I lived closer, but my waist is happy I don't.

The signature Bacon Bun is where it's at, but getting your hands on one after 11 a.m. can be a bit of a challenge since it sells out fast. Your best bet is to call ahead and reserve them. But if you get there and it is sold out, you can't go wrong with the maple bacon doughnut, cinnamon roll, strawberry holy cross bun, or the lemon meringue pie.

5

THE DUCK INN

THE DUCK INN, located in a former pre-Prohibition tavern, is a charismatic, trip-worthy destination for gratifying, chef-crafted New American cuisine and unique duck dishes. Chef-owner Kevin Hickey has a special connection to the neighborhood: Hickey and his family have lived in the neighborhood for generations, back to and including his great-grandparents. The restaurant is named after a diner Hickey's great-grandmother owned during the 1930s, where she served spaghetti, hamburgers, hot dogs, and tamales. Opening a restaurant in Bridgeport was not in his original plan, but everything fell into place, bringing him back to his roots.

The space is cozy and full of character with a retro-style bar, bright stools, gold orbit-like lights, a large backyard patio, and a sizable duck mural (*of course!*). With a name like The Duck Inn, well . . . you have to order the duck. The signature Rotisserie Duck is thoughtfully prepared, which is no surprise since Hickey worked in fine dining for two decades. The legs and thighs are injected with brine and roasted for several hours, while the breast is pan-roasted separately to medium-rare. The carved duck is served over duck-fat potatoes

TIP

Secret Menu Item: Try the **Up & Over** burger, their version of the In-N-Out burger with two large patties, American cheese, lettuce, pickles, and house-made sauce sandwiched between two plump potato buns. Dare I say it's better than In-N-Out? You'll have to try it for yourself.

and seasonal vegetables with a side of duck jus reduction. Another not-to-be missed item is the Duck Fat Dog. It has all the classic ingredients of a Chicago-style hot dog, like yellow mustard (no ketchup allowed), sweet relish, onions, tomatoes, pickles, hot peppers, celery salt, and a poppy seed bun but it's made with an all-natural beef-and-duck-fat dog. With one snappy bite, you'll see why this encased meat has received so many accolades.

It's not all 'bout the duck . . . 'bout the duck. The seasonal menu features a little bit of everything. From comfort food to seafood to meat to tasting menu, you can create your own palatable experience.

Start your meal with the Spanish Octopus, artfully plated with black walnut romesco, cucumber, ink aioli, and Meyer lemon. For something more audacious, try the crispy sweetbreads with field beans, serrano hot sauce, bread and butter pickled strawberries, and Wonder bread puree.

6

26TH STREET SUGAR SHACK

Craving sweets? Get your sugar fix at **26TH STREET SUGAR SHACK**, a beloved family-owned ice cream shop. This seasonal "shack" is best known for their Funnel Cake Sundaes, homemade Italian ice, hand-scooped ice cream, and treat-filled Blizzards. The lines can get a little insane, but waiting is worth the sugar rush.

Customer favorites are the deep-fried Funnel Cake Sundaes. What's there not to like about deep-fried morsels of goodness topped with vanilla soft serve, garnishes of your choice, whipped cream, and a cherry? If you're concerned about your summer bod, get the Mini Funnel Cake, but in my opinion, bigger is better. The Orange Creamsicle is exactly how you'd imagine: orangey, creamy, and oh, so gleamy! It will take you back to eating that familiar ice cream bar from your childhood. Speaking of childhood, one of my favorite treats growing up was Italian ice. There is nothing more refreshing than chomping on flavored ice during a sweltering summer day. The Italian ice here is house-made and comes in several flavors, including strawberry, lime, and mango. For a little fun factor, try the Ice Cream Taco because . . . who am I kidding? I'll take ice cream in any form.

THE PILSEN CRAWL

1. Crown your pie at **PLEASANT HOUSE PUB**, 2119 S. HALSTED ST., #1, CHICAGO, (773) 523-7437, PLEASANTHOUSEPUB.COM

2. Take the cake at **KRISTOFFER'S CAFÉ & BAKERY**, 1733 S. HALSTED ST., CHICAGO, (312) 829-4150

3. Fly high at **S.K.Y.**, 1239 W. 18TH ST., CHICAGO, (312) 846-1077, SKYRESTAURANTCHICAGO.COM

4. Drink, eat, and be merry at **DUSEK'S BOARD & BEER**, 1227 W. 18TH ST., CHICAGO, (312) 526-3851, DUSEKSCHICAGO.COM

5. Travel to Vietnam at **HAISOUS VIETNAMESE KITCHEN**, 1800 S. CARPENTER ST., CHICAGO, (312) 702-1303, HAISOUS.COM

6. Caffeinate yourself at **CÀ PHÊ DÁ**, 1800½ S. CARPENTER ST., CHICAGO, (312) 702-1303, CAPHEDACHI.COM

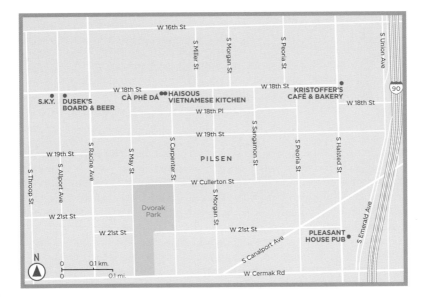

Pilsen

Food Works of Art

NEIGHBORHOODS DON'T GET MORE AUTHENTIC THAN PILSEN. When you stumble upon its artsy vibe, you will experience outdoor murals in the most creative, fun, and tasteful places—on the sides and facades of buildings, "L" stations, underpasses, signs, and just about anywhere you can imagine. Once a port of entry for many immigrants, first the Germans, Irish, and the Bohemians in the 1800s, then the Mexicans, who came to the area in the 1900s around the time of the First World War, due to labor shortages. Pilsen preserves and celebrates the Mexican heritage and culture every day, but their marquee event is the Fiesta del Sol—a four-day festival in July when over a million annual attendees celebrate Mexican culture, food, and music. Pilsen's rich history is still evident from the many other ethnic eateries, which celebrate the cultures that helped build this great neighborhood.

1

PLEASANT HOUSE PUB

PLEASANT HOUSE PUB is a beer-centric public house known for fanciful royal pies, bloody good British-inspired food, wicked pastries, and energizing brews and drips brought to you by husband-and-wife duo Art and Chelsea Jackson. This Michelin's Bib Gourmand destination is an expansion of their Pleasant House Bakery, where they first introduced their prized royal pies and pastries to Chicago.

The flaky, buttery pastry is scrumptious with just about any filling. You will find traditional-style pies like the Steak & Ale, filled with rich, flavorful beef stew, or unique creations like the Chicken Balti with chicken, tomatoes, and aromatic curry spices. Mushroom & Kale is a vegetarian option with a creamy white-wine and Parmesan sauce that can be enjoyed equally by carnivores. Crowning your pie is a thing here; top it with a scoop of mashed potatoes and gravy. If you're into gravy, the Deluxe Gravy Chips will tickle your fancy. Thick potato wedges are doused with the savory gravy and topped with braised beef and aged cheddar. The Bangers & Mash is a hearty meal with house-made sausages, fluffy mashed potatoes, and onion gravy that will leave you all warm and fuzzy inside.

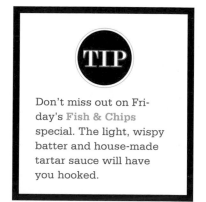

TIP

Don't miss out on Friday's **Fish & Chips** special. The light, wispy batter and house-made tartar sauce will have you hooked.

2

KRISTOFFER'S CAFÉ AND BAKERY

Sometimes it's hard to distinguish where the "best" of something is served, but I indisputably say the best tres leche cake can be found at **KRISTOFFER'S CAFÉ AND BAKERY.** According to Kristoffer's Facebook page, even Rick Bayless claims it's the best. If Bayless says it's good, you know it's good.

Owners Luis and Martha Figueroa bought the business from the initial owners 15 years ago and kept the original tres leche cake recipe we know and love today. It is so popular that a good portion of their sales come from other restaurateurs who buy it to serve at their own businesses. Made with three types of milk, the cakes are handmade in small batches by Martha every day. The best sellers are vanilla, caramel, coconut, and Kahlúa. Specialty flavors like eggnog make seasonal appearances. Another star on the menu is the Chocoflan. Making it is laborious, as the cake and flan are made separately, yet once the mixtures are poured together, enchanting layers of moist cake and rich flan are created right before your eyes. The drinks at Kristoffer's are also made from scratch with individual attention. Cool down with an Iced Horchata Latte during hotter days and warm up with a Mayan Hot Chocolate on colder ones.

3 S.K.Y.

S.K.Y. serves an Asian-inspired menu influenced by chef-owner Stephen Gillanders's extensive travels. The initials represent his wife's name, Seon Kyung Yuk, who designed the space on a small budget. Gillanders worked for Jean-Georges Vongerichten for over a decade and then came to Chicago to work at Intro, the former Lettuce Entertain You restaurant. He originally planned on opening a restaurant in his hometown of Los Angeles but fell in love with the vibe in Chicago and decided to open his first venture in Pilsen, home of several exceptional restaurants.

Grab a predinner drink at the intimate lounge up front by the entrance. The Seon Daze (sake, vermouth, turmeric, lemon) and seasonal cocktails are fruity and refreshingly light. Follow the kitchen light as you walk through a narrow pathway to enter the main dining area. The menu is easy to navigate and broken out by Snacks & Shares, Appetizers, Mains, and Vegetables. Start off with the Black Truffle Croquettes, explosive, crunchy little bites of aged white cheddar and jalapeño. The Hamachi Sashimi has an alluring textural and visual contrast with thick pieces of hamachi, diced avocado, crunchy puffed rice, sprinkles of black sesame, and drips of chili oil and ponzu sauce. Maine Lobster Dumplings come submerged in

jade butter and enhanced with soft herbs. Gillander describes the Organic Fried Chicken as Japanese *karaage* meets Nashville hot, but with his own twist: The creamed corn sauce is poured tableside. Complete the meal with one of pastry chef Tatum Sinclair's signature desserts, like the Chocolate Whiskey Pie nestled atop fluffy marshmallow with coffee gelato.

4 DUSEK'S BOARD & BEER

DUSEK'S BOARD & BEER is a cornerstone of the neighborhood, a crowd favorite for a chill night of drinking and eating, a high-energy spot for gathering and socializing. The focus is on beer, food paired with beer, and creating fond memories around beer. Located inside the musical landmark Thalia Hall, Dusek's is the only Michelin-starred restaurant with a live band venue attached to it. With a huge passion for music, managing partner Bruce Finkelman shares that this and all the other concepts in the 16″ on Center hospitality group are places he would want to hang out.

At the front is the hopping bar area, and in the back, a relaxed dining room. The seasonal menu is enlightening and atypical of bar food. Creative delicacies range from Country Pâté to Black Truffle & Foie Gras Fondue, fresh oysters, and the unforgettable Iron Roasted Mussels with smoked pimento and warm harissa butter.

The Asparagus and Crab Salad looks like a spring version of a Christmas wreath, with strategically placed arugula, frisée, fennel, tarragon sabayon, and croutons surrounding a golden sun of confit egg, all with lemon dressing. The Slagel Farm Truffle Honey Glazed chicken dish is delightfully fancy, glazed with truffle honey and combined in the most tasteful way with artichoke *barigoule*, roasted fingerling potato, niçoise olives, quail egg, and preserved orange–green peppercorn vinaigrette. Fried chicken is so last year; here it's all about the Chicken Fried Rabbit. It was my first

time trying, and it definitely won't be my last. Throw down a thirst-quenching beer and order a plate of the Choucroute ("sauerkraut" in French) with seared duck breast, duck sausage, confit duck leg, confit potatoes, and natural duck jus.

HAISOUS VIETNAMESE KITCHEN

HAISOUS is a breath of fresh, aromatic air. Chef Thai Dang and his wife Danielle provide authentic Vietnamese food with overflowing passion and pureness while breaking the barriers that perceive Asian cuisine as cheap food. HaiSous, meaning "two pennies" in Vietnamese, is representative of the partnership between the two and the dream they built with just two pennies. Vietnamese-born chef Dang cooks food from the heart and sticks to the familiarity of his culture but with fine-dining techniques that are indicative of his background and training. The dishes are well composed and flawless, with all the warmth of mom's cooking.

There's a true feel of hospitality and homeness to the place. Danielle, who is an architect by trade, designed the space using handmade furniture from Vietnam to create an inviting place where you just want to hang. She also oversees the beverage program, and the drinks are not to be missed. You'll find revivifying concoctions with vodka, pomegranate juice, Velvet Falernum, and lemon, or a digestif cocktail with coffee, fernet, cocoa nib–infused tequila, and egg white.

Goi, meaning "salad," is quintessential to Vietnamese dining. Gỏi Bạch Tuộc features octopus, confit eggplant, coconut cream, roasted peanuts, and shaved radish, while the Gỏi Sò Điệp highlights smoked bay scallops, pomelo, lime, shallots, and Thai chile. What is sensational about both dishes are the aromatic herbs and the balance of sweet, spicy, salty, and tangy. Out of the specialty meat dishes, fried chicken wings and pork chop is fantastic, and the roasted duck stuffed with kaffir lime leaves is cooked to perfection. Vegetarian dishes are handled with love as well. Just look at the Mì Chay with egg noodles, which stands like a sculptural piece of art and garnished with Chinese broccoli, and shiitake mushrooms.

6

CÀ PHÊ DÁ

The owners of Hai-Sous opened **CÀ PHÊ DÁ**, a Vietnamese cafe located next door, serving Vietnamese coffee, street food, sandwiches, phở, and more. There is a big coffee culture in Vietnam; it is second only to Brazil in coffee consumption. Cà Phê Dá translates to "iced coffee" in Vietnamese. The specialties here are drip-filtered coffee drinks sweetened with condensed milk made from products imported from chef Thai Dang's family in Vietnam. Ordering the Cà Phê Dá, which can be made hot or cold, is a given. Pair your drink with one of their sweet pastries, like the Coconut Bun with coconut cream and longan strawberry jam. The bright green color of the freshly baked Pandan Brioche will catch your eyes and your heart.

Slather on the coconut jam to enhance the subtle floral and nutty flavors.

This ultracasual counter-service spot is ideal for a quick bite any time of the day. It caters to restaurant workers in the neighborhood and stays open until midnight, Monday through Saturday. The Vietnamese Bánh Mì sandwiches start off with a house-baked baguette and are layered with chicken pâté, protein of choice, sliced cucumbers, pickled papaya, and fresh herbs. With bold and fragrant flavors, the Phở is unlike anything I've had in Chicago. There is no chintziness in quality or quantity. The Cơm Gà ("chicken rice") is absolutely delicious and vibrantly flavored.

Bonus Crawl!

The Pilsen Taco Crawl

Keep calm and have a taco. The Pilsen Taco Crawl pays homage to the families who have kept the traditions of the Mexican culture in the neighborhood.

THE TACO CRAWL

1. **TAQUERIA TAYAHUA**, 2411 S. WESTERN AVE., CHICAGO, (773) 247-3183

2. **5 RABANITOS**, 1758 W. 18TH ST., CHICAGO, (312) 285-2710, 5RABANITOSDOTCOM.WORDPRESS.COM

3. **CARNITAS URUAPAN**, 1725 W. 18TH ST., CHICAGO, (312) 226-2654, CARNITASURUAPANCHI.COM

4. **TAQUERIA LOS COMALES**, 1544 W. 18TH ST., (312) 666-2251, LOSCOMALES .COM

5. **CARNITAS DON PEDRO**, 1113 W. 18TH ST., (312) 829-4757

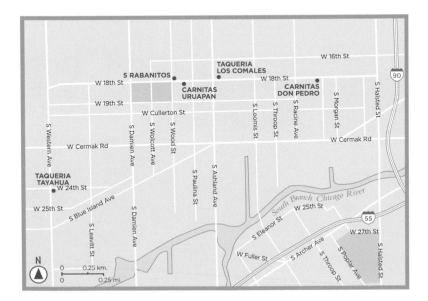

1

TAQUERIA TAYAHUA: TACOS EN CARBON

You may walk or drive right pass **TAQUERIA TAYAHUA** since it doesn't look like much from the outside, but it is a hidden gem that specializes in food from the Mexican state of Zacatecas. Pedro Almaraz opened the restaurant in 1992 and chose this neighborhood because he lived and worked nearby. He frequently passed the building where his restaurant now stands. When he saw the FOR SALE sign, he immediately jumped at the chance and bought it. Currently, his son, Rolanda Almarez, runs the business and carries on the traditions of his father, maintaining the feel of the neighborhood. When you walk in, the space seems small, but there is plenty of room, with extra seating in the back.

The menu features a wide range of items, including breakfast, soups, seafood, dinner entrees, burritos, tortas, and more. So, essentially you can come for a traditional Mexican meal any time of day. The tacos are a crowd favorite, but they are truly known for their Tacos En Carbon, which are cooked over charcoal, giving them a smoky taste. Charred rib eye, grilled onions, jalapeño, and beans are jam-packed into a handmade corn tortilla. Squeeze on the lime and take the biggest bite you can.

5 RABANITOS: COCHINITA PIBIL TACOS

Chef-owner Alfonso Sotelo named **5 RABANITOS** (meaning "five radishes") with his family in mind. Before coming to the States, Sotelo lived in Guerrero, Mexico, where his family grew radishes. He and his four brothers would go into town to sell the radishes, and people referred them as the "*cinco rabanitos*." Sotelo worked for Rick Bayless in the kitchens of Chicago's Topolobampo and Xoco for 19 years before opening his own restaurant. He chose Pilsen, a block away from the National Museum of Mexican Art, because he wanted a business that served the Hispanic community.

The menu features food from various regions of Mexico while incorporating the flavors of his hometown. Everything is prepared fresh with a varied selection to fit one's taste, even catering to vegetarians with a dedicated menu. The tacos are priced under $3 and come with your choice of filling: Pork al Pastor, Pibil, Chorizo, Carnitas, Chicken Tinga, Carne Asada, Beef Barbacoa, and Roasted Vegetables. They are simply dressed with onion, cilantro, and, not surprisingly, radishes. The Cochinita Pibil Tacos are unique since most restaurants in Chicago don't make *cochinita pibil*, a traditional Yucatán-style pork slow-roasted in acidic juices and seasonings and wrapped in banana leaves. The tacos are topped with pickled onions and finished with cilantro. The meats are all well-seasoned and really speak for themselves. I know we came here for the tacos, but really we stay for everything else.

3 CARNITAS URUAPAN: PORK CARNITAS TACO

Follow the smell of slow-cooked pork right through the doors of **CARNITAS URUAPAN**. The menu is exclusively dedicated to carnitas and a few traditional side dishes that complement the juicy meat, including *chicharrones* (because who doesn't need pork on pork?), cactus salad, and refried beans.

Inocencio Carbajal emigrated from Uruapan, Michoacán, to the United States in the late 1960s to pursue the American dream. He worked at meatpacking plants in the West Loop and saved every penny he had to open Carnitas Uruapan in 1975. He decided to open in Pilsen, right across from Chicago's first Mexican supermarket, where he was known to approach people coming out of the store with a taco. Carbajal has since retired, but his son Marcos runs the family business and carries on the traditions his father built from day one. You know they have something special when you still see lines out the door. The people who have come here since the beginning are now bringing their kids and their kids' kids. It's a place where generations have enjoyed—and will enjoy—the food for many more years to come.

Carnitas are a labor of love, cooked for hours in rendered fat, resulting in flavorful, tender meat. All parts of the pig are used and devoured. No heavy sauce is needed; these are best enjoyed with the house-made salsa. The spice from the jalapeño and acidity of the vinegar balances out the fattiness of the pig. The carnitas are available by the pound or per taco. Either way the portions are massive for the price, so come pig out! Pun intended.

TAQUERIA LOS COMALES: TACOS DE LENGUA

Camerino Gonzalez always wanted to have his own business, and through his hard work and dedication, he opened a quaint restaurant in the 1970s known as **TAQUERIA LOS COMALES**, where he served authentic Mexico City–style tacos in a casual atmosphere. His first location was in the South Side of Chicago and expanded to numerous other locations, including Pilsen as well as surrounding suburbs. All restaurants are independently owned and run by family members.

The idea is simple: Create fast, tasteful dishes using premium ingredients while upholding the culture of Mexican cuisine in a family-oriented environment. The menu showcases tacos, tortas, burritos, combination platters and more. Please note each location may have a different menu. The tacos are available in familiar meats, like Bistec Chopped Steak, Al Pastor Pork, Saudero Flank Steak, Chorizo Mexican Sausage, Barbacoa Shredded Beef, Cecina Seasoned Steak, and Pollo Abobado Marinated Chicken, all served with cilantro and onions. Less familiar but popular are the Tripas (beef tripe) and Lengua (beef tongue). The beef tongue is a very tender meat if cooked properly, and Los Comales does it right. Add their homemade salsa for a little spice. The tacos are slightly smaller than normal size, but that just means you can try more.

5 CARNITAS DON PEDRO: TACOS DE CHICHARRÓN AND TACOS DE SESOS

Walk this way to porkin' heaven. **CARNITAS DON PEDRO** is a low-key, no-frills restaurant with a menu centralized on carnitas, a traditional dish from the city of Michoacán, Mexico, where founder Eduardo Duarte is from. He chose to open in 1981 in Pilsen, where he resided. Currently, Magdalena Duarte (daughter) and Eduardo Duarte (son), both named after their parents, help run the business. The carnitas are rendered in their own fat, which takes about 3 hours and results in a distinctive meaty taste and pull-apart texture. Choose from white or dark meat, ribs, skin, stomach, or a mix. Traditionally, the meal is enjoyed on the weekends in a group environment, bringing together family and friends. With that said, you will find long lines on the weekends. The prices are super affordable, and you can feed a whole family for under $20.

They only serve pork, and it's available all year-round. Every part of the pig is used, right down to the skin and brains. It's chopped to order and available per pound or per taco. The Taco de Chicharrón (pork rinds) is cooked in a mild salsa, adding richness, and served with a cilantro and diced onion mixture, pickled jalapeños, lime wedges, and a stack of warm corn tortillas. Build to your liking and enjoy. The Sesos, aka "brains," may not be top of mind, but if you are feeling adventurous give it a try. Carnitas Don Pedro's version is served in a fried taco shell stuffed with the seasoned and sautéed *sesos*; it's available only on the weekends. With a tofu-like consistency, it tastes a little like liver, but it's not as strong.

THE CHINATOWN CRAWL

1. Warm up at **LITTLE SHEEP MONGOLIAN HOT POT**, 2342 S. WENTWORTH AVE., CHICAGO, (312) 929-3224, LITTLESHEEPHOTPOT.COM

2. Roll on over to **LEGEND TASTY HOUSE**, 2242 S. WENTWORTH AVE., CHICAGO, (312) 225-8869, LEGENDTASTYHOUSE.COM

3. Lift noodles at **XI'AN CUISINE**, 225 W. CERMAK RD., CHICAGO, (312) 326-3171, XIANCUISINECHICAGO.COM

4. Dim sum and then some at **MINGHIN CUISINE**, 2168 S. ARCHER AVE., CHICAGO, (312) 808-1999, MINGHINCUISINE.COM

5. Stay up late at **CHI CAFE**, 2160 S. ARCHER AVE., CHICAGO, (312) 842-9993, CHICAFEONLINE.COM

6. Bake the world a better place at **SAINT ANNA BAKERY & CAFE**, 2158 S. ARCHER AVE., CHICAGO, (312) 225-3168

7. Treat yourself at **JOY YEE NOODLE** and **JOY YEE PLUS**, 2139 AND 2159 S. CHINA PLACE, CHICAGO, (312) 842-8928, JOYYEE.COM

8. Fill up on **QING XIANG YUAN DUMPLINGS**, 2002 S. WENTWORTH AVE., STE. 103, CHICAGO, (312) 799-1118, QXYDUMPLINGS.COM

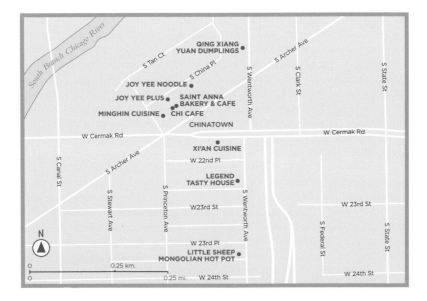

Chinatown

Dumplings and Noodles and Bubble Teas, Oh My!

LET'S FACE IT, IF YOU ARE A FOOD LOVER and a city has a Chinatown, you have to go. Can you say pork bun, egg tart, and dim sum? While Chicago's Chinatown may not be as historic or expansive as San Francisco's or New York's, it is one of the largest in North America and will not disappoint. Chinatown has always been one of my favorite neighborhoods in the city, but after marrying into a Chinese family, I now frequently visit. Getting there is really easy by train (Red Line), by boat (Chicago Water Taxi), and by car. Aside from the lunchtime crowds on the weekends, parking is readily available.

Chicago's Chinatown is broken up into two sections: Main Chinatown and Chinatown Square. The original Main Chinatown is easy to spot by the iconic Chinatown Gate at Cermak and Wentworth. Head south on Wentworth as there is a lot to see. Chinatown Square, a short stroll to the north of the gate, runs along Archer Avenue and features a two-story "mall" full of shops, bakeries, and restaurants. While many people head there for gifts, herbs, and tea shopping, I focus on the food, *obvi*! In addition to traditional Chinese cuisine, there has been a recent surge of other Asian restaurants opening, including a Thai rolled ice cream spot. You should definitely take it all in and walk both the old and new sections. It can sometimes get a little confusing on where to eat, but luckily you have this book.

1

LITTLE SHEEP MONGOLIAN HOT POT

Nothing says "sharing is caring" like a hot pot dinner where everyone gathers around a communal pot of boiling broth and dips a selection of fresh meats, seafood, and vegetables. The simmering pot of aromatic soups steams your face and opens up your pores. As you sip on the chile oil– and spice-infused base, sweat will drip down the side of your head; it's an experience of its own but one better shared with others. And remember, more people = more food.

LITTLE SHEEP MONGOLIAN HOT POT specializes in Mongolian-style hot pot, which is traditionally served in round metal pots and cooked at the table. First choose your base: original, spicy, or half-and-half. If you like variety, go for the half-and-half. Next, select your protein. They have a large assortment to choose from, including fresh seafood and premium meats. The most popular is the thinly sliced lamb meat, which I saw on almost every table—including mine! Finally, pick your veggies and starch. They have a bunch of different

types of vegetables, including napa cabbage, baby bok choy, pea sprouts, and enoki mushrooms, as well as several types of noodles and dumplings.

There is no right or wrong way to enjoy hot pot. I've seen people cook each ingredient individually, while others combine everything together at the same time. To each their own.

TIP

Recommended cook time for thinly sliced meats is about 10 to 15 seconds, or until the meat changes color; green vegetables around a hot 1 to 2 minutes; and everything else in 3 to 5 minutes.

2 LEGEND TASTY HOUSE

Thai rolled ice cream shops have been popping up in Chicago during the last few years, but the best place to get your hands on one is at **LEGEND TASTY HOUSE**. This "ice pan" or "stir-fried" ice cream originated in Thailand with street vendors and became popular in neighboring countries like Cambodia, Malaysia, and the Philippines. The United States caught on shortly after, and now people can't get enough of these trendy treats.

It starts off in a liquid form and is poured onto a chilled steel pan with fruit, cereal, or other ingredients for flavor. The mixture is combined until the liquid solidifies into a creamy texture. The ice cream is then flattened into a square, scraped into rolls with a metal spatula, and placed in a cup with your favorite garnishes; select from various toppings like gummy bears, jelly beans, Pocky sticks, fresh fruit, and cookies. The possibilities are endless. Sweet dreams are made of this.

I usually lean toward anything green tea, so my go-to is the Green Tea Queen with green tea rolled ice cream, fresh strawberries, whipped cream, marshmallows, green tea syrup, and green tea Pocky. *Tea-rrific!* Go bananas over the Monkey Business with Nutella rolled ice cream, fresh bananas, whipped cream, jelly beans, caramel sauce, and chocolate Pocky. The Perfect Pair with mango and strawberries is pure *pair-fection*.

XI'AN CUISINE

3

XI'AN CUISINE is in a league of its own when it comes to northern Chinese cuisine. The menu is simple, with a focus on small dishes, hand-stretched noodles, flavorful flatbreads, and specialty soups. As you walk in, the scent of the bone broth and fragrant spices fills the air of this low-key restaurant.

The must-order item on the menu is the lamb flatbread. The consistency of the warm bread is spot-on, with a crackling exterior and chewy interior. The pockets are packed with unsparing amounts of cumin-spiced minced lamb. The lamb broth with hand-stretched noodles is a classic dish, though different from other restaurants' versions in Chinatown. The long, wide, hand-pulled noodles accompany the white, milky broth, creating a dish that is sincerely comforting and soothing. All the noodle dishes are fantastic, since they take the time and effort to carefully craft them to precision. The stir-fried wide noodles and lamb skewers are consistently good. Eating at Xi'an Cuisine is easy and low-pressure, like you're eating at your own family's home.

MINGHIN CUISINE

Dim sum is typically enjoyed during brunch or lunch over a pot of tea. Drinking tea encourages conversations with others and helps promote digestion throughout your meal. When it comes to *yum cha* ("drink tea" in Cantonese), **MINGHIN CUISINE** is all that and *dim sum*. From the ornate decor, with the hanging crystal chandeliers, to the superb food options, it's an excellent choice when you want an elegant place to gather with friends and family

to share small plates of steamed, pan-fried, deep-fried, and baked goodies.

My husband is Chinese, so many of our family gatherings include dim sum. I leave the ordering to the experts—my in-laws—as the menu and all its options can seem a little overwhelming. My sister-in-law and I love Har Gow (shrimp dumplings), so there's always plenty of that on the table. They usually get me my own order, because I can be a little *shellfish* when it comes to the shrimp dumplings.

MingHin serves dim sum 365 days a year from 8 a.m. to 4 p.m., and starting back up from 9 p.m. to 2 a.m.

The Siu Mai is very popular with the family, too. MingHin's version is filled with pork and shrimp and wrapped with thin wonton dough that is shaped with pleated edges. My nephews love the steamed BBQ Pork Buns, and rightfully so. The soft, pillowy buns are filled with bountiful barbecue pork at MingHin. Hubby loves the Stir-Fried Rice Noodles with Beef, Chinese Broccoli with Oyster Sauce, and Sticky Rice, in which the glutinous rice is mixed with chicken, egg yolk, and Chinese sausage, wrapped in a dried lotus leaf, and steamed. These remind my husband of his childhood, because his mom made these dishes all the time. I think we all tend to gravitate toward food we remember eating, like mom's cooking, and dim sum is always a memorable family affair. End the meal with their Baked Creamy Egg Yolk Bun!

5

CHI CAFE

We've all been there before—that late night drinking with friends, scrambling to find good eats at 2 a.m. **CHI CAFE** is the spot for you. They are open until 4 a.m. Sunday through Thursday and 24 hours on Friday and Saturday. *Yasssss!* Even better, the broad menu has an assortment of classic Chinese dishes at super-reasonable prices. *Double yasssss!*

If you need some carbs to soak up the alcohol, opt for one of their noodle or rice dishes. The Beef Egg Noodles or Special Fried Rice is the perfect hangover cure. Live life with a little spice and order the Sichuan Shrimp, which is packed with generous portions of shrimp, vegetables, and a bit of heat. The Mini Wok soups are great for the winter months. One of the most popular dishes on the menu is Sizzling Beef, served in a blazing-hot cast-iron pan. This food is one thing you won't regret the next day.

6

SAINT ANNA BAKERY & CAFE

This no-frills, traditional Chinese bakery serves some of the best baked goods in the city. The display case is filled with colorful cakes, savory and sweet buns, custardy tarts, coconut-coated mochi, and other delectable creations. Every trip I make to Chinatown includes a stop at **SAINT ANNA BAKERY & CAFE** for a box of goodies.

People are obsessed with the oval-shaped Egg Tarts. The sweet, custard-like center is wrapped in a flaky crust. The baked BBQ Pork

Buns are filled with sweet yet savory pieces of meat that pairs oh, so perfectly with the buttery bun. The light butter cream in the Coconut Bun is worth all the calories, and the cushiony sponge cake has just the right amount of sweetness. Classics like the Banana Nut Bread are straightforward but addictive. A lot of the smaller businesses in Chinatown are cash only, including Saint Anna.

7

JOY YEE NOODLE AND JOY YEE PLUS

If you see a long line in Chinatown Square during the summer time, it's most likely people waiting for a thirst-quenching bubble tea smoothie at **JOY YEE NOODLE**, a popular pan-Asian restaurant. They were the first to introduce Chicago to Taiwanese-style bubble teas, and their version started the trend of natural fruit freezes combined with *boba* (tapioca balls). The menu is massive, with various options to customize your drink to your liking. From exotic fruits to jellies to mini pearls to coffee, you will need the time in line to strategize what you want.

Enjoy a bubble tea smoothie at the restaurant, where they serve large portions of pan-Asian cuisine or get one to go at the bubble tea station right by the entrance. During warmer weather, they have a walk-up window with limited hours. Walk a few doors down to their shabu-shabu restaurant, **JOY YEE PLUS**, where they serve ice cream bubble waffles and specialty teas. The photo-worthy chai tea, s'mores, and Strawberry Festival desserts are divine.

Joy Yee Plus also features unique teas that come in cute packaging. Ever had a cheese tea? Don't fear—there aren't gobs of mozzarella in your tea. Instead, a fluffy and creamy cheese-flavored foam sits atop the tea. If you are not feeling adventurous, get a regular fruit tea, like the revivifying Four Season Fruit Tea.

8 QING XIANG YUAN DUMPLINGS

QING XIANG YUAN DUMPLINGS, or as most of us like to call it QXY Dumplings (way easier to pronounce), serves fresh, crescent-shaped soup dumplings. Everything is made to order from scratch. You can watch the dumpling connoisseurs assemble these delightful pockets of juicy concoctions through a glass window in the back of the restaurant. It's handmade, it's legit, it's the real deal.

Once you are seated, the server hands you an iPad, where you can peruse the extensive menu while your mouth waters from the smell of the dumplings and your stomach growls in anticipation. But you'll need to focus, because decisions need to be made. The dumpling section of the menu is separated into different categories, including Chef Special Dumplings and various proteins (beef, chicken, lamb, pork, and seafood) as well as a decent-size vegetarian section. Each category has different flavor profiles, with added ingredients like leeks, mushrooms, dill, cabbage, carrots, and celery to name a few. It's all just preference. Then decide how you would like it prepared: boiled, steamed, or panfried. Finally, how many can you throw down? Minimum order is 12 pieces, and the better value is 18.

The boiled dumplings are on the doughier side than steamed or fried ones but tend to do a better job keeping the delicious broth inside. The lamb and coriander, a Chef Selection item, has a distinctive taste, with a slight tartness from the Chinese parsley. My favorites are the steamed dumplings, which come out in a traditional bamboo steamer; they have the perfect dough-to-meat-to-soup ratio. Try the Chef's Special Jadite Dumplings with natural green coloring, and pork and cabbage. The panfried dumplings are fantastic as well, but everything tastes better fried. *Right?* Try the beef and onion combo, too.

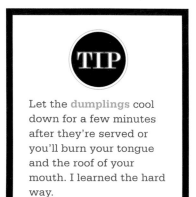

TIP

Let the dumplings cool down for a few minutes after they're served or you'll burn your tongue and the roof of your mouth. I learned the hard way.

THE SOUTH LOOP CRAWL

1.   Fine dine it up at **ACADIA**, 1639 S. WABASH AVE., CHICAGO, (312) 360-9500, ACADIACHICAGO.COM

2.   Belly dance at **KURAH MEDITERRANEAN**, 1355 S. MICHIGAN AVE., CHICAGO, (312) 624-8611, KURAHCHICAGO.COM

3.   Be cheesy at **THE SCOUT WATERHOUSE + KITCHEN**, 1301 S. WABASH AVE., CHICAGO, (312) 705-0595, THESCOUTCHICAGO.COM

4.   Get your hands dirty at **LOWCOUNTRY**, 1132 S. WABASH AVE., CHICAGO, (888) 883-8375, LOWCOUNTRYCHICAGO.COM

5.   Scream for ice cream at **GORDO'S HOMEMADE ICE CREAM BARS**, 729 S. DEARBORN ST., (312) 461-1116, GORDOSICECREAM.COM

6.   Lunch a bunch at **CAFECITO**, 26 E. CONGRESS PKWY., (312) 922-2233, CAFECITOCHICAGO.COM

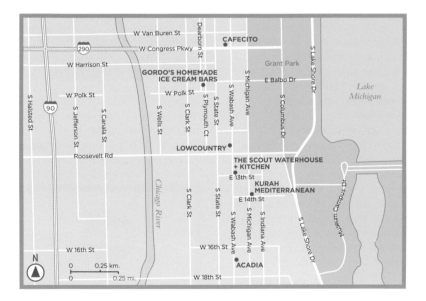

South Loop

South Your Mouth

THE SOUTH LOOP IS LOCATED SOUTH OF THE LOOP (yep, you guessed it!) and was one of Chicago's first residential districts. The boundaries are often debated, and many even argue the South Loop is no longer a Chicago neighborhood but rather an amalgamation of Central Station, Dearborn Park, Museum Campus, Near South Side, and Printer's Row. I'm a (food) lover not a fighter, so I have wrapped all of those "neighborhoods" together as the South Loop. The experts can debate, and I will focus on the eats.

Although working class immigrants originally settled the area, many businesses migrated south from the Loop after the Chicago Fire of 1871. Decades later, in the 1950s and '60s, a decline of passenger and freight trains and changes in the printing businesses left the South Loop vacant. In the 1970s, developers drove the resurgence of the South Loop as a residential hub, which continues today. Beyond "up and coming," the South Loop has a great blend of converted loft spaces and new, trendy residential developments. It is also home to Chicago's Museum Campus, where you will find famous attractions like the Adler Planetarium, Field Museum, McCormick Place, Shedd Aquarium, Soldier Field, and some really great restaurants.

1

ACADIA

Tucked away off the beaten path on Wabash Avenue between 16th and 18th Streets sits a Michelin two star–rated restaurant, **ACADIA**. Chef-owner Ryan McCaskey opened the doors in 2011 and has won numerous accolades through the years, including a Michelin star less than a year after opening. In 2015, he was awarded two Michelin stars and has retained the honor since then. McCaskey combines his classical training and modern approach to create phenomenal dishes that will enlighten your senses. He draws inspiration from Maine, where he has spent time since his childhood. The space is calm and tranquil, with a minimalist decor that lacks the stuffiness that comes with some fine-dining experiences.

Acadia's main dining serves a tasting menu with ever-changing dishes based on seasonality and sourcing. Wine pairings are available for an additional charge. Each elegantly prepared dish is meticulously plated with attention to every detail, while the layers of flavors are playful and awe-inspiring. A Thai *tom kha*–inspired broth is poured onto the Stonington lobster with daikon, kohlrabi, and kaffir lime, which brings warmth with a little zest. The Aleutian Islands king crab with yuzu pearls and parsley root is served with mint-ramp water, creating a cool, invigorating dish. One bite into the Wagyu beef topped with fresh uni, and I was in heaven: The different and contrasting textures from the melt-in-your-mouth beef, creamy uni, gelatin-like egg yolk, and doughy pancake that sat as a base all worked together harmoniously. Vegetarian options are also available. In season was a beautiful garden of peas and carrots prepared in various ways and topped with pea shoots and brightly colored edible flowers. Pastry chef Kyleen Atonson brought out her funnel cake with Greek yogurt *crémeux*, an impressive structure of poached green rhubarb, verjus grapes, pickled green strawberries, green almonds, and candied almonds. Her desserts are not overly sweet and have a savory element. At Acadia, presentation is as important as taste and quality.

2 KURAH MEDITERRANEAN

At the corner of 14th Street and Michigan Avenue, you will find **KURAH**, a family-owned restaurant serving well-prepared Mediterranean food made with organic meats and produce. The atmosphere is cozy and intimate, with brightly patterned walls and ornate decorative accents. The owners also own the South Loop Market and have close ties to the neighborhood. They grew up in the area and have seen firsthand the development and expansion through the years.

Kurah is a full-service restaurant with a stocked bar, so grab a drink. Cocktail options include the Pomegranate Mojito (white rum, sparkling white wine, and pomegranate juice over muddled lime and mint), Tequila Rosé (Massya Lebanese Rosé, tequila blanco, raspberry jam), and Clementine Martini (clementine vodka, Pellegrino Aranciata, and fresh orange). The Honey Old Fashioned is a customer favorite, with

Town Branch bourbon, honey, pomegranate syrup, and bitters. Also available are beer, wine, and other libations.

Start your meal with the red lentil soup, which is an olive oil–based soup with carrots and parsley. Every dish is made in-house, fresh every day. The hummus is a must-order signature dish drizzled with homemade cilantro–pine nut dressing and garnished with fresh Persian cucumbers and juicy tomatoes. Dip liberally with the fluffy pita. Sweetness, saltiness, and a little bit of tanginess is what you will experience when you bite into the bacon-wrapped dates. The sizable dates are encased in applewood smoked bacon and submerged in pomegranate syrup. Any of the grilled kebab platters are a win, especially the well-seasoned Black Angus beef rib eye served with saffron basmati rice and your choice of grilled veggies or Jerusalem salad. They also offer halal meats as well as plentiful gluten-free, vegan, and vegetarian options.

Enjoy live entertainment including belly dancers (ooh!), contortionists (aah!), knife throwers (eek!), and other rotating acts the first Friday of each month.

THE SCOUT WATERHOUSE + KITCHEN

Cheer on your favorite sports team at **THE SCOUT WATERHOUSE + KITCHEN**. Get your game face on at this upscale sports bar where large flat-screen TVs line the walls and the drinks keep a'flowing. There's an extensive beer list available in draft and bottles, as well as a large selection of wine and cocktails. Kick back and relax after work with The Gramercy Manhattan and your choice of Bulleit Bourbon or Templeton Rye, sweet vermouth, simple syrup, and grapefruit bitters. Spice things up with a Tortuga Martini, a revitalizing mix

of Patrón Reposado, St-Germain, pink grapefruit juice, and fresh lime juice garnished with red hot chile peppers.

As a food-driven sports bar, they serve killer bar food. The menu is chef-crafted and inspired by American classics like mac and cheese, burgers, sandwiches, and salads. Nothing says comfort food like a gooey grilled cheese, and The Scout's versions are a foot long. Yup, a whole foot of cheesy goodness! The signature Triple Cheese grilled cheese is made with nine slices of three different kinds of cheeses sandwiched between two long slices of buttery brioche. It comes with a side of steamy tomato basil dip for your dunking pleasure. They also have a few other variations of the ginormous grilled cheese, like the braised short rib version with mozzarella, provolone, sautéed peppers, and onions, which is their unique spin on the classic Philly cheesesteak sandwich. The Scout is known for their nachos, and they're great for sharing. The Pulled Chicken Nachos come loaded with chicken tinga, pico de gallo, sour cream, guacamole, and roasted tomato salsa. You can also substitute short rib, if you'd prefer. The house-smoked and oven-roasted prime rib takes about four hours to make and is served sandwich-style in a rustic baguette with caramelized onions, mushrooms, and swiss cheese; dip amply into the warm au jus and enjoy.

4 ... LOWCOUNTRY

Get your hands dirty and face messy at **LOWCOUNTRY** because eating seafood out of a bag never tasted

so good. It's all about the Cajun-style seafood here, set in a relaxed, backyard vibe with picnic tables and embellished greenery. An outdoor affair wouldn't be an outing without drinks, and Lowcountry's are cold, stiff, and downright invigorating. You must try the Perfect Highball, made with Suntory Whisky Toki and effervescent water, which is 150 percent as carbonated as champagne. Get in vacation mode with the Rum Punch, a fruity mixture with rum served in a tiki glass. You will easily rosé the day away with the Rosé Sangria, with slices of fresh peach and lime, pomegranate, and tequila. If you want a spiked lime soda, the limeade with Ford's gin, lime, and house-made basil syrup will quench your thirst.

Now it's time to get low. Pick your protein: shrimp (head on or off), snow or king crab legs, mussels, lobster tail, and crawfish all priced by the pound. Choose your sauce: Cajun spice, lemon pepper, garlic, or "everything." Determine your heat level: weak sauce, hot, very hot, and ridiculously hot. (I love my spice, and I'm usually good with very hot.) Finally, select your add-ons: corn on the cob, red potatoes, and andouille sausage. It comes in a clear bag, and you eat directly out of it. No silverware needed here, but bibs and gloves are optional.

For sides, a popular item is the Soft-Shell Crab fried whole in a light batter. The full-flavored Garlic Noodles have a robust garlic taste, so you might not want to eat them on a first date, and the Fried Green Tomatoes with pimento cheese are addictive. End your meal with Deep-Fried Oreos. Need I say more?

HOW TO EAT BOILED CRAWFISH

1. Pinch the tail with your thumb and index finger.

2. Twist the head and detach it from the body with your other hand. You can suck the juices from the head, if desired.

3. Separate the tail from the body.

4. Twist the end of the tail and slowly wiggle it out to devein.

5. Peel the shell off the body and enjoy the meat.

GORDO'S HOMEMADE ICE CREAM BARS

Customized ice cream bars are the specialty at **GORDO'S HOMEMADE ICE CREAM BARS**, which shares a space with its sister restaurant, Flaco's Tacos, a taqueria serving fresh Mexican eats. The owners, Jim and Ed Hebson (brothers) and Jim Masterson (cousin), named the dessert shop "Gordo's" since the Spanish *flaco* translates to "skinny," and *gordo* to "fat." Get it?

The ice cream is made on-site and takes a great deal of effort and time to create. I've watched the process myself, and there is no cutting corners here. Each flavor is laboriously crafted and refined by hand. Enjoy the bars on their own, or create your dream bar in three easy steps: pick, dip, and sprinkle. Pick your ice cream bar flavor, like dulce de leche, Oreo, mint chip, butter pecan, coffee, and more. There also are nondairy options

available, such as avocado banana, hibiscus tea, and orange chile spice. Dip it in your choice of chocolate (white, milk, and dark) or caramel. Sprinkle with nuts, cereals, or candy bars. The possible combinations are limitless.

The mint chip bar is splendid with white chocolate dip, crumbled Oreos, and dark chocolate drizzle. Dip the chocolate bar in milk chocolate dip and top it with Butterfingers and dark chocolate drizzle for a divine chocolate treat. Now say that five times. Happiness on a stick is generally topped with rainbow confetti sprinkles, so add generously. Strawberry milk bar and Fruity Pebbles is reminiscent of eating strawberry milk and cereal as a child. Wait? You didn't do that? The buttery and nutty butter pecan bar goes well with the white chocolate dip, peanuts, and a milk chocolate drizzle.

6

CAFECITO

Looking for an easy and affordable lunch spot in the South Loop? Look no more. **CAFECITO**, a counter-service restaurant, offers distinctive Latin American eats and coffee with one of the best Cuban sandwiches in the city. There are multiple locations citywide, all with a casual ambience and friendly service. Pressed sandwiches, specialty salads, house-made soups, and large platters are featured on the menu, with a strong focus on using fresh, all-natural ingredients. The Cubano is outstanding, and if you've never had one here, you definitely need to try it. Thin slices of pork marinated in their homemade *mojo*

(citrus, garlic, cumin, and spices), cured ham, swiss cheese, mustard, and pickles are all wedged between two firm pieces of bread. The combination is pressed together on a grill like a panini, which locks in all the flavors, creating the ultimate sandwich.

For a heartier meal, try the traditional platters. All the platters come with white rice, black beans, plantains, and your choice of protein. Options include grilled shrimp, sliced steak, braised beef, sautéed tilapia, and more prepared with different sauces. The Guava-Q Pork is a crowd favorite, with roasted pork and caramelized onions cooked in a sweet, guava barbecue sauce. It comes with a side of jicama slaw, a nice alternative to the traditional cabbage slaw.

You saved room for dessert, right? If you did, grab one of the guava pastries, cheesecake, or a Mexican wedding cookie. Get a caffeine boost with a concoction of Cuban or American coffee. I like getting the Cuban coffee and churros, a version of the traditional coffee and doughnuts. If you didn't save room, you can always go back for more. Desserts can be eaten any time of day, multiple times a day. Or is that just me?

Breakfast sandwiches are served from 7 to 11 a.m. A popular item is the Huevos Chimichurri Breakfast Sandwich, layered with light and fluffy scrambled eggs, tangy chimichurri, and sliced tomatoes.

THE LITTLE ITALY & UNIVERSITY VILLAGE CRAWL

1. Keep it simple at **JIM'S ORIGINAL**, 1250 S. UNION AVE., CHICAGO, (312) 733-7820, JIMSORIGINAL.COM

2. Wine and dine at **DAVANTI ENOTECA**, 1359 W. TAYLOR ST., CHICAGO, (312) 226-5550, DAVANTIENOTECA.COM

3. Beef up at **AL'S BEEF**, 1079 W. TAYLOR ST., CHICAGO, (312) 226-4017, ALSBEEF.COM

4. Chill out at **MARIO'S ITALIAN LEMONADE**, 1066 W. TAYLOR ST., CHICAGO, (312) 201-6760, MARIOSITALIANLEMONADE.COM/MARIOS_ITALIAN_LEMONADE/SHOP/HOME

5. Stuff your face at **FONTANO'S SUBS**, 1058 W. POLK ST., CHICAGO, (312) 421-4474, FONTANOSSUBS.COM

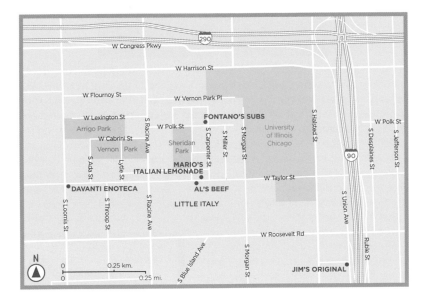

Little Italy & University Village

Rooted in Traditions

CHICAGO'S NEAR WEST SIDE, the neighborhood west of the South Loop, has been known as Little Italy since the early 1900s. Once the center of Chicago's Italian-American community, it is still well known for its authentic Italian eateries along and around Taylor Street. If you have been to Italy, you understand visiting *duomos*—the Italian term for "church" or "cathedral"—in just about every city. So when you're in Chicago's Little Italy, make sure to visit the Shrine of Our Lady of Pompeii—the oldest continuing Italian-American church in Chicago, which was built in Roman revival style and known for its stained glass, wall and ceiling murals, and high arches among the pews.

Since 1963, Little Italy has also been known as University Village, after the opening of the University of Illinois at Chicago (UIC). This combination of Italian culture and active student life makes for an energetic neighborhood with plenty of tasty culinary options. In Little Italy/University Village, you will find traditional Italian pastas and pizzas as well as Chicago classics, like Chicago dogs and Maxwell Polish Sausages, and new restaurants designed to appeal to the diverse student population.

1

JIM'S ORIGINAL

JIM'S ORIGINAL has been open since 1939 and tells the story of the late Jim Stefanovic, who immigrated to Chicago from Duf, Macedonia (formerly Yugoslavia). He worked at his aunt's hot dog stand, located on the corner of Halsted and Maxwell Streets. Eventually, in 1941 he bought it from his aunt, who was sick at the time, with the money he saved from selling taffy apples. In spite of a few relocations, Jim's Original is the longest-operating hot dog stand that opened from the original Maxwell Market. You will immediately know you've landed at Jim's Original from the smell of the sweet grilled onions that encompasses the space. Follow the scent to the walk-up window.

In 1941, Stefanovic created the Maxwell Street Polish Sausage Sandwich, a well-prepared encased sausage smeared with mustard and packed in with grilled sweet onions. In 1947, he introduced the Pork Chop Sandwich, a bone-in pork chop with mustard and grilled onions. Most of the menu items still come with mustard and grilled onions, including the Double Cheeseburger with two patties and American cheese. But you can't go to a hot dog stand and not get a hot dog, so double the fun and get yourself a Double Vienna Beef Hot Dog. It's places like Jim's Original that are the heart of Chicago.

Everything on the menu is $7 and under, with tax included. All sandwiches come with fries at no additional charge.

DAVANTI ENOTECA

Carbs and wine are always a good idea, and **DAVANTI ENOTECA** is a darling spot to enjoy both. Modern takes on traditional Italian dishes and rustic vibes make it a desirable place for any social gatherings. Diners can enjoy shareable plates in an inviting setting, surrounded by exposed brick walls lined with bottles of wine and warm service. Grab a drink at the crowded bar or steal a peek at the open kitchen. Either way take it all in.

The menu is broken into several categories, including Sfinci (Cravings), Antipasti (Appetizers), Insalata (Salads), Pizza, Pasta, Pesce (Fish), Per la Tavola (For the Table), and Carne (Meat), so there's a little bit of something for everyone's taste. Start off with the meatballs, a blend of prosciutto and veal braised in San Marzano tomatoes and topped with pecorino and ciabatta. Food Network named them some of the best meatballs from coast to coast. Soak the bread with every inch of the hearty sauce. Give a toast to the Truffle Egg Toast, a thick cut of toasted bread laid over a bed of chopped asparagus and coated with melted fontina cheese, with

two egg yolks with truffle oil huddled on top. When it comes to the Crispy Brussels Sprouts (prosciutto, chiles, pecorino, and egg), executive chef Peter DeRuvo incorporates a nice balance of acidic, savory, and spicy elements, and the sunny-side up egg binds everything together and creates a yolky sauce.

For the table, you must get the Focaccia di Recco, a Lingurian-style flatbread stuffed with soft cow's cheese and served with a sticky, gooey piece of honeycomb. The sweet and salty combo with the warm doughy focaccia is heavenly. I know you don't usually

think of a burger when you go to an Italian restaurant, but you need to try the Davanti Burger, one of Eater.com's 20 Most Essential Chicago Burgers. The juicy beef patty, a mixture of sirloin, chuck, and brisket, is stacked with grid-dled cheese curds, arugula, and roasted tomatoes, and smeared with bacon jam and roasted garlic aioli. You get a smokiness from the bacon without having an actual piece of bacon. The thin-cut, crispy Parmesan fries are habit-forming in all the right ways. Unbutton your pants now because you still have dessert on the way. A substantial scoop of maple gelato sits atop a warm Brown Butter Blondie and is drizzled with caramel sauce and garnished with chopped Marcona almonds.

Shhhh!
Check out chef DeRuvo's secret menu item, Pasta alla Deruvo, a luxurious caviar carbonara with truffles!

AL'S BEEF

If you are a true Chicagoan, you'll have a deep appreciation for an Italian beef sandwich, especially at the iconic **AL'S BEEF**. The legendary sandwich was invented by a group of Italian immigrants during the Great Depression, when meat was scarce. The roasted meat was sliced really thin, dipped in its juices, put in thick loaves of Italian bread, and served mostly at weddings. There's much debate on which family first introduced the sandwich, but the Ferrari family was the first to open an actual beef stand. In 1938, Al Ferrari started one because he wanted a place for bookies to gather. It was opened just at night, and there was no gas, only charcoal, so it was originally called Al's Bar-B-Q. Ferrari created the original recipe along with his sister and brother-in-law, Frances and Chris Pacelli Sr., in Al's kitchen, and it's the recipe they still use today. What was once a small food stand has turned into a quintessential Chicago staple, with franchise locations across the United States.

So what makes a good Al's Beef? First comes the bread, a soft French bread from Gonnella Baking Company, which holds its structure and stands up to the beef gravy. Then comes the beef, a dry-roasted USDA-certified top sirloin roast cooked in a proprietary blend of pure spices and natural juices. Next comes the au jus, aka "gravy," made with natural ingredients and no chemicals, which gives it a distinctive taste. Finally add your toppings. The traditional way is to top it with Al's secret house-made giardiniera, which is not overly spicy but has enough heat to bring out the flavors of the meat. They also have sweet peppers, cheese, and an Italian sausage, which is chargrilled right in the store.

GET YOUR AL'S BEEF SANDWICH IN FOUR LEVELS OF JUICINESS:

Regular—Just enough beef gravy is added so the bread still holds all the juice.

Wet (most popular)—Additional beef gravy is added with a little juice dripping down your hand.

Dipped—The entire sandwich is submerged in the gravy, with juices pouring down your hand. You'll need to roll up your sleeves for this one.

Dry—The boring way to eat it. Don't do it!

4 MARIO'S ITALIAN LEMONADE

An iconic spot for cool treats on a hot summer day is **MARIO'S ITALIAN LEMONADE**, a seasonal stand featuring frozen Italian lemonade. Mario's has been a Chicago staple since 1954 and continues to draw crowds, with lines down the block every summer from May to September. Mario DiPablo Jr., along with his parents, Mario Sr. and Dorothy DiPablo, opened the shop when lemonades were hand-cranked and sold for two cents. Mario DiPablo Jr. still runs the show today, together with his wife and grown children. DiPablo Jr. stays true to the family's traditions with the original recipes as well as the look and feel of the stand, a promise he made to his dad. DiPablo Jr. is a humble man who doesn't own a cell phone or use technology and still sweeps the floors outside the stand. Although many people approach him to expand, he doesn't want to franchise because he wants there to be only one Mario's.

The lemonade flavors are written on each side of the walk-up window. The DiPablos originally started with lemon, and it's still the most popular flavor today. A slushy pile of ice can be filled with a rainbow of other flavors including blue raspberry, pomegranate, pineapple, fruit cocktail, piña colada, and more. They are served in random cups that DiPablo Jr. has bought from businesses that have closed. He prefers not to have his name on the cups, because he doesn't want to pass on the extra costs to the customers since, in reality, we all go for the lemonade and not the packaging.

5

FONTANO'S SUBS

FONTANO'S SUBS is an old-school sub shop that has been open since 1960. The Little Italy location was the first, where it all began for the Fontano family. Word traveled fast about their fantastic sandwiches, and it was named Chicago's #1 sub sandwich by the late Pat Bruno, the *Chicago Sun-Times* food critic, as well as "The Best Sandwich Shop in the Nation" by Zagat in 2012. The sub shop is also part supermarket, selling traditional Italian products including meats, cheeses, sauces, and more.

Subs come in 6, 8, 10, 12, and 16 inches. The meatballs in their Meatball Sub, the most popular, are made with ground beef, pork, and bread crumbs and mixed with special house spice and eggs. Some other Fontano favorites are the Blockbuster, busting out with ham, Genoa salami, capocollo, provolone, and swiss cheese; the Wise Guy, layered with prosciuttini, capocollo, Genoa salami, and provolone; the Caputo, stuffed with pepperoni, capocollo, Genoa salami, and provolone. You have the option to add hot or mild giardiniera, pickles, cucumbers, and/or other fixings for no additional charge. All the sandwiches are fully loaded, messy, and pure *carb-licious*.

Meatball Challenge

Eat a 3-foot meatball sub with 18 meatballs and 18 slices of provolone cheese in under an hour and receive the sandwich for FREE, plus a $50 Fontano's gift card and T-shirt. Will you be on the Wall of Fame or Wall of Shame? Balls to the wall.

Dine communal at **AVEC**, 615 W. RANDOLPH ST., CHICAGO, (312) 377-2002, AVECRESTAURANT.COM

Experience the goat at **GIRL & THE GOAT**, 809 W. RANDOLPH ST., CHICAGO, (312) 492-6262, GIRLANDTHEGOAT.COM

3. Share Italian fare at **FORMENTO'S** and **NONNA'S**, 925 W. RANDOLPH ST., CHICAGO, (312) 690-7295, FORMENTOS.COM; NONNASCHICAGO.COM

4. Double the fun at **SMYTH** and **THE LOYALIST**, 177 N. ADA ST., CHICAGO, (773) 913-3773, SMYTHANDTHELOYALIST.COM/SMYTH; SMYTHANDTHELOYALIST.COM/THE-LOYALIST

5. Quench your thirst at **THE AVIARY**, 955 W. FULTON MARKET, CHICAGO, (312) 226-0868, THEAVIARY.COM

6. Get boisterous at **ROISTER**, 951 W. FULTON MARKET, CHICAGO, ROISTERRESTAURANT.COM

7. Take flight at **ORIOLE**, 661 W. WALNUT ST., CHICAGO, (312) 877-5339, ORIOLECHICAGO.COM

8. Surf and turf at **SWIFT & SONS** and **COLD STORAGE**, 1000 W. FULTON MARKET, CHICAGO, (312) 733-9420, SWIFTANDSONSCHICAGO.COM; COLDSTORAGECHICAGO.COM

West Loop

Best Loop, West Loop

CHICAGO FOOD LOVERS SAY WEST LOOP IS THE BEST LOOP, and it is hard to argue. Since the original seven restaurants opened on Randolph Street in the 1990s, earning it the name "Restaurant Row," no other area has seen such a fast or diverse growth of culinary options. Oprah opening Harpo Studios in the West Loop helped start the transformation. Today, the West Loop boasts five Michelin star–rated restaurants and other establishments led by signature chefs such as Grant Achatz, Rick Bayless, Bill Kim, Stephanie Izard, and Noah Sandoval. Recently, new employers like Google, McDonald's, and Uber opened offices in the West Loop, and this confluence of restaurants and corporations makes it one of the most desirable places to live and eat in Chicago.

The West Loop's history has long been about food. When Fulton-Randolph Market opened in 1850, Randolph Street Market was focused on produce, while Fulton Market, 2 blocks to the north, was the home of meatpacking, and Carl Sandburg claimed Chicago was the "hog butcher for the world." These markets have since been replaced by Chicago's hotbed of new restaurants. And while Fulton Market's meatpacking has virtually gone by the wayside, the meatpacking and warehouse vibe is still part of the West Loop's charm.

1

AVEC

The West Loop has been home to **AVEC** (One Off Hospitality Group) since 2003, and it continues to be a crowd favorite for a cozy and intimate dining experience. It is one of the original restaurants that gave Randolph Street the name "Restaurant Row." The narrow space is minimalistic, with sleek lines and contemporary-style wood covering the walls, ceilings, and floor. A pioneer in communal dining, Avec's ambience is still centered on sharing and gathering together around long tables.

The original concept was for a wine bar, but Avec quickly gained fame for its amazing food. Wine still remains a big part of the menu, with a focus on small producers from Greece, France, Italy, Spain, and Portugal, all priced under $90 per bottle. Chef Perry Hendrix oversees the rustic food menu, which is centralized around small plates. Hendrix uses seasonal Midwest ingredients with a Mediterranean flair that is inspired by his extensive travels. You can find sizable chorizo-stuffed Medjool dates with a spicy piquillo pepper–tomato sauce, or dazzling hummus with wood-oven baked pita. The Deluxe "Focaccia" looks overly simple, but the flavors are quite complex. The round focaccia is shaped and cut like pizza and topped with velvety Taleggio cheese and ricotta. Did I mention the truffle oil? Excuse me while I shovel this down.

2 GIRL & THE GOAT

Let me fangirl for a second—I love Stephanie Izard. This Chicago-born superstar chef, mom, and all-around nice person was the first woman to win Bravo's *Top Chef* (Season 4). **GIRL & THE GOAT** opened as part of the Boka Restaurant Group in 2010 and was one of the first restaurants established in the Randolph restaurant corridor. It is still one of the toughest reservations to secure, so book ahead, way ahead.

From the dynamic bar on the left to the main dining area on the right to the open kitchen across the back wall, the atmosphere is electrifying. The menu is categorized by vegetable (V), fish and seafood (F), and meat (M)—a little something for everyone. Dishes are small-plate format and meant to share. Everything lives up to the hype, including the vegetable dishes. The Sautéed "Magic" Green Beans in fish sauce vinaigrette with cashews will disappear in two seconds. Your heart will beat for the roasted beets with green beans, white anchovy, and avocado *crème fraîche*, topped with bread crumbs. Under Fish/Seafood, the Hamachi Crudo is a winner, with chile-soy vinaigrette and puffed rice, or the seasonal Softshell "Crab Cake" with a tangy mayo and soy glaze. Braised beef tongue and duck tongues appear on the meat side, as does the signature Wood Oven Roasted Pig Face. Braised and wood-fire roasted, the pig face comes topped with fried potato stix and a sunny-side up egg. If you're not feeling that adventurous, the Ramp Marinated Grilled Chicken is a safe bet.

TIP

Goat legs are available for preorder; call the restaurant in advance to add them to your reservation.

3

FORMENTO'S/
NONNA'S

FORMENTO'S (B. Hospitality Company) is an Italian restaurant named after co-owner John Ross's grandmother "Nonna" Formento, built on family traditions yet set in a contemporary atmosphere. Ross shares that his fondest food memories growing up were around his nonna's cooking. Up to 50 family members would gather weekly to feast on her homemade creations. The menu plays homage to her recipes, like Nonna's Meatballs, a tried-and-true classic, while incorporating modern techniques from executive chef Todd Stein.

Stein does an excellent job of creating palatable dishes that speak to him and the neighborhood while maintaining the warmth of Ross's fond childhood memories. Lightness and flavor are the main focuses, and nothing is overly done or heavy. The extremely gratifying bucatini is a simple

preparation of carbonara, pancetta, egg yolk, and black pepper. Vivid colors pop from the green chiles, mint, and tomatoes in the Chitarra, a squid ink pasta dish. Well-prepared seafood and meats are available on the menu, including a grilled whole branzino topped with bright pea tips and crispy garlic chips. No meal is complete at Formento's without the chocolate cake, Nonna's recipe with dark chocolate mousse and hazelnut praline. Ross says he always wants this cake on his birthday.

Accessible through the entrance of Sangamon Street, Formento's sister restaurant **NONNA'S** serves made-to-order sandwiches, soups, salads, pizza, and homemade desserts. Get the famous Nonna's Meatball Sub or a piled-high Chicken Parmesan Sub. When it comes to the Sicilian-style pizza, everyone's a winner and gets a crispy corner piece.

4 SMYTH AND THE LOYALIST

Although the names **SMYTH** and **THE LOYALIST** are used as one and the same, they are two contrasting concepts with completely different personalities. Husband-and-wife team John Shields and Karen Urie Shields, both Charlie Trotter alums, opened the duo notion in 2016. The two restaurants occupy the same building, one upstairs and one downstairs. Upstairs is Michelin two star–rated Smyth, an upscale fine-dining establishment with a tasting menu; downstairs is laid-back and loungy The Loyalist serving elevated bar food.

The name "Smyth" is a nod to the farmlands of Smyth County, Virginia, where the couple lived for five years and opened a restaurant called Town House. The vibe of Smyth is warm, as if you were in a friend's open-concept kitchen. Three tasting menus are offered with varying course numbers driven by ingredients from The Farm, a 20-acre farm located an hour south of the city. The menu changes with the season, offering dishes like fava beans with aromatic herbs and buttermilk, or Gulf shrimp with malted cream and fermented white asparagus.

The Loyalist is the home of one of the best burgers in the city, even named one of the top three burgers in the country by *Bon Appétit* magazine. Nicknamed the "Dirty Burg," it's a burger you won't mind getting

messy for. The menu here is also driven by the seasons and The Farm, but it's more casual and approachable. You will find lighter fare like raw oysters or the Leek Mimosa with sunflower butter and potato. Although the word *mimosa* doesn't reference the brunch drink you're used to, you can get a breakfast-inspired dish like the omelette with Camembert and marinated morels. Substantial offerings, like a steak dinner or pasta, are available as well.

5 THE AVIARY

Chef Grant Achatz's **THE AVIARY**, an Alinea Group concept, is a posh cocktail lounge that takes a fine-dining approach to alcoholic beverages, with innovative drinks and a five-star experience. The mixologists are trained as chefs, and the ingredients used are thoughtfully sourced. Acclaimed for its "molecular gastronomy," The Aviary features innovative and intricate cocktails that are just as enjoyable to watch being made as they are to drink. Cedar smoke fills the bird's nest of the Back Taxy, giving off a deep, earthy aroma. Although the elements might change slightly, this particular mixture of the Back Taxy was made with genmaicha green tea, cranberry, winter wheat, and sloe gin. "Cereal Killer," a dark drink, appears in a puffy, plastic Aviary bag Then the server cuts open the bag to release smells that are reminiscent of Cinnamon Toast Crunch; inhale while sipping on the Maker's Mark Private Select bourbon made especially for The Aviary. The most iconic and recognizable cocktail is the one that comes in the porthole, where the booze is infused with different fruits, herbs, spices, and more. Small bites are available for purchase, including the salt-and-vinegar Crispy Pork Skins with a spiced corn dip.

The grand experience does come with an extravagant price, but it is like no other. No phone number is listed, so you can't call to make a reservation. Instead you buy tickets, as you would for a concert, via their online booking system, Tock. A 7-course Kitchen Table Experience, 5-course Cocktail Tasting Menu with paired food, 3-course Cocktail Progression, and à la carte are the various options. No changes are allowed once booked, so make 100 percent sure the date and time work for you.

6

ROISTER

ROISTER, a casual restaurant from the Alinea team, has different vibes from the other restaurants in the group. Compared to the other concepts, the atmosphere here is boisterous and the menu accessible with attainable prices. The main dining room sits in the front of the space, while the open kitchen (with a wood-fired oven) is perched in the back. Snag a counter seat that surrounds the kitchen and watch the chefs fire it up.

Although the restaurant is more laid-back, it still strives to provide a high standard of excellence in every detail of its cooking. The food is inspired by all cultures, and the evolving menu showcases global ingredients. For instance, the Japanese A-5 Quarter Pounder with cheddar, mushrooms, and special sauce is pure melt-in-your-mouth goodness. It is a bit of a splurge at $53 for a single patty and $100 for a double, but worth every penny. The famous Fried Chicken Sandwich won't break the bank, but it tastes like a million bucks with sunchoke hot sauce and chamomile mayo. Boring toasts are of the past. Get an upgrade with the Cinnamon Toast slathered with foie gras mousse and strawberry jam. Foie gras comes in candy bar form, too, with black walnuts, pretzels, and caramel. Feel like a kid again with a big bowl of Cookies and Milk, chocolate-chip cookie dough and milk ice cream. Not everything on the menu is super indulgent. Balance it all out with their salad offerings, such as the Cobb Salad.

7 ORIOLE

ORIOLE is a hidden gem, literally tucked away in a back-alley-like street. On my first attempt to find the restaurant, I was dropped off in the middle of nowhere, wondering if I was at the right place. Once you find the unmarked door and enter the premises, a staff member greets you and then takes you through a freight elevator. *Abracadabra!* The elegant, 28-seat dining room is revealed, home to the Michelin two star–rated restaurant. The intimate setting is not what you would typically expect from a fine-dining establishment with a lofty feel, exposed brick, and open kitchen.

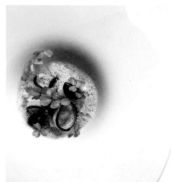

Executive chef–owner Noah Sandoval's tasting menu isn't designated to one type of cuisine but offers an exploration of diverse flavors and clever plays on textures. Envision perfectly placed, luxurious golden osetra caviar laid atop cured hamachi and floating on a pond of dill and saffron. The seared Hudson Canyon scallops swim in a bubbly foie gras emulsion and are topped with pickled cherry and oxalis. Little specks of puffed brown rice sprinkle the grilled little gem, which accompanies the buttery Japanese A5 Wagyu beef. Pastry chef Courtney Kenyon's presentation of the Mignardises, cute little bonbons, tarts, cream puffs, and doughnuts, is delightful.

8

SWIFT & SONS AND COLD STORAGE

Get the best of both worlds at 1000 West Fulton Market where land meets sea. A joint effort by Boka Restaurant Group and B. Hospitality Company, **SWIFT & SONS** is an upscale steakhouse where meats are aplenty, while **COLD STORAGE** is the informal raw bar within it. Fulton Market, formerly known as the meatpacking district, was where American steak got started. In the 19th century, Gustavus Franklin Swift Sr. founded one of the most lucrative trades in the Midwest: the cattle industry. These two restaurants take inspiration from Swift with a new world approach, while conserving some of its history.

Executive chef Chris Pandel commands the kitchen at both restaurants. Pandel focuses on high-quality Midwestern ingredients and refined techniques, indicative of his training and background. Prime cuts of meat at Swift & Sons include filet, New York strip, Australian Wagyu, porterhouse, bone-in rib eye, and more. While the steaks are the highlight of the menu, it's not all about the beef. You can get fresh shellfish piled on a bank of ice, or a well-prepared fish dish like the Grilled Loup de Mar with baby lettuce and basil pistou. A Thai-inspired soup, classic salads and sides, and seasonal pasta are also featured. Cheers to all the delectable food and refreshing cocktails.

Situated in what was once Fulton Market cold storage facility, **COLD STORAGE** centers on seafood in a laid-back environment, perfect for socializing over drinks. Pandel brings the finest seafood from the East and West Coasts and the Great Lakes. There's plenty of fish in the sea with bountiful Shellfish Towers, whole Grilled Branzino, Fish & Chips, and Seafood Tins. Save room for the Narwhal sundae with eight scoops of ice cream.

$1 oysters and $3 beers, Monday through Friday from 3 to 6 p.m.

Bonus Crawl!

The Best Desserts in the West

I want a good body but not as much as I want desserts. The West Loop is filled with splurge-worthy spots that shouldn't be missed. Here are a few of my favorite spots.

THE WEST LOOP DESSERT CRAWL

1. **WARM BELLY BAKERY**, 1148 W. MONROE ST., CHICAGO, (312) 265-0780, WARMBELLYBAKERY.COM

2. **CONE GOURMET ICE CREAM**, 1047 W. MADISON ST., CHICAGO, (312) 666-5111, CONECHICAGO.COM

3. **PARLOR PIZZA BAR'S DESSERT DEALER**, 108 N. GREEN ST., CHICAGO, (872) 315-3005, PARLORCHICAGO.COM

4. **BOMBOBAR**, 832 W. RANDOLPH ST., CHICAGO, (312) 967-7000, BOMBOBAR .COM

5. **VANILLE PATISSERIE**, 131 N. CLINTON ST., CHICAGO, (773) 868-4574, VANILLEPATISSERIE.COM

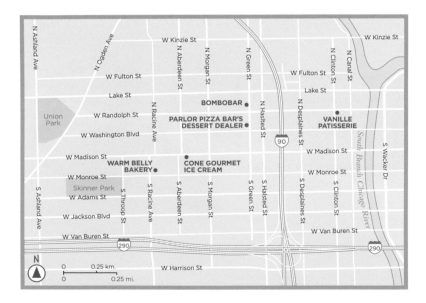

1 WARM BELLY BAKERY

Cofounder and CCO (chief cookie officer) of **WARM BELLY BAKERY**, Joe Dela Pena says cookies have always been his thing ever since he was a kid, but he never conceived he would open a cookie shop. His background was in education, but he always had a passion for baking. He isn't a classically trained chef but got started by making cookies as a hobby for friends, catering jobs, and weddings. Now he is a celebrity is his own right and has been featured in numerous publications as well as making appearances on various television shows.

What makes these cookies so irresistible? They are whimsical and nostalgic with creative twists on traditional flavors. The texture is close to cookie dough and very substantial: a quarter pound of cookie. Premium ingredients are used and flavors are inventive. They'll warm your belly and your heart. Choices include classics like Chocolate Chip, S'mores, and Apple Pie as well as global flavors like Mexican Hot Chocolate, Ube, and Matcha. Assortments of cereal cookies are available as a shout-out to Momofuku Milk Bar. Every day is your birthday with the Birthday Cake cookie.

2 CONE GOURMET ICE CREAM

CONE GOURMET ICE CREAM is a family-owned scoop shop serving Irish-themed treats, gourmet ice cream, European-style soft serve, build-your-own sundaes, and more. Born and raised in Ireland, owner Sean McGuire has been bringing magically delicious treats from his hometown into the West Loop neighborhood since 2013. The Shamrock cone is one of the signature items and combines two childhood favorites, ice cream and Lucky Charms, because cereal is not just for breakfast anymore.

You can choose to build your own sundae or try one of their special creations. The ice cream flavors are intriguing, like the Netflix and Chill with popcorn ice cream and M&Ms, or the Leprechaun Tracks with peanut butter cups, fudge, and vanilla. Sundae Fun-days are well spent eating a Blarney Turtle Sundae topped with caramel, hot fudge, roasted pecans, house-made whipped cream, and a cherry on top. For a dairy-, soy-, and gluten-free option, try the Sorbetto Slushie made with your choice of sorbet and Club Rock Shandy. For the ultimate splurge, get the brioche bun stuffed with PB&J ice cream, a fun twist on a classic.

3

PARLOR PIZZA BAR'S DESSERT DEALER

DESSERT DEALER is the dessert counter located next to the main entrance of Parlor Pizza Bar, specializing in sweet tacos, soft serve, and baked goods. Enter to find one of the prettiest desserts on Instagram, the TACOlato (taco + gelato). Make sure your camera eats first. You'll Go Nuts (chocolate gelato with Nutella, hazelnuts, and Ferrero Rocher) and even B-A-N-A-N-A-S (banana fudge gelato, bananas, peanut butter cups, crushed peanuts, and peanut butter sauce) for the Caramelo Anthony (salted caramel gelato, caramel sauce, chocolate-covered pretzels, Rolos, and whipped cream in a white chocolate shell). Unicorn Dreams do come true with birthday-cake ice cream topped with candy and marshmallows in a confetti-sprinkle shell. If you have a specific flavor combination in mind, BYOT (build your own taco) by picking your taco shell, gelato or ice cream, sauce, and three toppings.

The menu also features desserts you never knew you needed in your life like the Fried Gelato, two mounds of fried salted caramel gelato covered with caramel, Cinnamon Toast Crunch, whipped cream, and slices of fresh strawberries.

4

BOMBOBAR

BOMBOBAR is a coffee and dessert walk-up window concept of Bar Siena, a DineAmic Group and chef Fabio Viviani restaurant. Indulge in splendid treats like the famous *bomboloni* (an Italian holeless doughnut), house-made gelato, specialty drinks, and more. Satisfy your sweet appetite seven days a week year-round whenever your cravings call.

The soft, fluffy bomboloni is topped with an adorable "Squeeze Me!" bottle to fill your doughnut with flavors such as raspberry, caramel, Nutella, and vanilla bean custard. You'll want to stuff it thoroughly to ensure you get enough filling in each bite. During the summertime, cool down with their #fromscratch gelato, which comes in unique flavors like pistachio, charcoal Oreo, Cookie Monster Dough, birthday cake, and lemon sorbetti. Top it off with sprinkles, cereal, candy, caramel, or Nutella. For colder months, warm up with a S'mores or Funfetti hotter chocolate—but before you sip in all the goodness, don't forget to take a photo of these Instagrammable treats. The S'mores comes with toasted marshmallows, graham crackers, and chocolate, while the Funfetti is topped with whipped cream, sprinkles, and Italian biscotti. These drinks are garnished with a cute mini bomboloni, because doughnuts and hot chocolate are meant to be.

5 VANILLE PATISSERIE

A dedication to the art of French pastry is evident at **VANILLE PATISSERIE,** with carefully crafted macarons, meticulously decorated cakes and cupcakes, and the attentively hand-made chocolates and pastries. Chef-owner Sophia Evanoff is dedicated to her craft, and her great commitment is shown through the quality, taste, and presentation of her desserts. The selection is a little limited at the French Market location, which is a condensed version of their shops, but the fine approach remains the same.

Vanille Patisserie is best known for their elegant macarons with a luscious, crisp shell sandwiching a chewy, emulsified filling. The spectrum of colors that lines the display case shelves reveals a multitude of flavors. It is hard to narrow them down to a few, but I went for the pistachio, coconut, lemon, raspberry, lavender, and vanilla. The filling is flavorful but not too overpowering and has the right balance of crunch to chew. You won't be able to resist the Stud Muffin, their popular cupcakes crowned with a signature macaron. Vanille (pronounced vah-NEE) means "vanilla" in French, so you can't go wrong with the Chad Stud Muffin, a white buttermilk cake filled with vanilla mousseline and topped with a vanilla macaron. For a *berry* good alternative, the Fraisier (strawberry) cake is delightful with a banana cake base, vanilla mousseline, passion-fruit curd, and fresh strawberries. If chocolate is more your thing, the Manjari, a flourless chocolate cake with dark chocolate mousse and dark chocolate glaze, is scrumptious. The Royal, with a crisp caramel streusel base, hazelnut dacquoise, chocolate mousse, and glaze, is glorious.

THE LOOP CRAWL

1. Fly with pigs at **COCHON VOLANT BRASSERIE**, 100 W. MONROE ST., CHICAGO, (312) 754-6560, COCHONVOLANTCHICAGO.COM

2. People watch at **THE GAGE**, 24 S. MICHIGAN AVE., CHICAGO (312) 372-4243, THEGAGECHICAGO.COM

3. Sweeten things up at **TONI PATISSERIE & CAFÉ**, 65 E. WASHINGTON ST., CHICAGO, (312) 726-2020, TONIPATISSERIE.COM

4. Take it easy at **THE DEARBORN**, 145 N. DEARBORN ST., CHICAGO, (312) 384-1242, THEDEARBORNTAVERN.COM

5. Eat meat at **PRIME & PROVISIONS**, 222 N. LASALLE ST., CHICAGO, (312) 726-7777, PRIMEANDPROVISIONS.COM

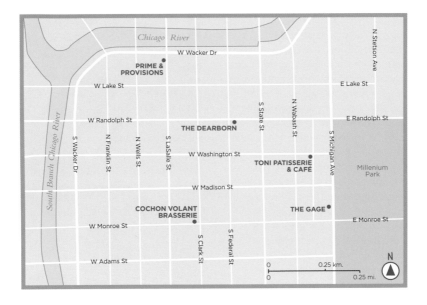

The Loop

Loop Around Town

DOWNTOWN CHICAGO IS KNOWN AS "THE LOOP," which is the central business district and civic center. While the Loop is home to Chicago's financial district, hundreds of companies both big and small, City Hall, and the Daley Center, it also has many popular tourist destinations, including the Art Institute of Chicago, Lyric Opera, River Walk, shopping on State Street, Theater District, and Willis Tower. A lot is packed into the populated 1.6 square miles bound by Lake Michigan to the east, the Chicago River to the north and west, and Congress Parkway to the south.

Amid the hustle and bustle and the crowded streets, the Loop is home to three of Chicago's top parks. Grant Park is known for Buckingham Fountain and large fields that are used for sport clubs as well as major city events, such as the Taste of Chicago, Lollapalooza, and the Chicago Marathon (start and finish). Maggie Daley Park along Lake Shore Drive offers a 3-acre playground, climbing wall, skating ribbon, miniature golf, and more. Millennium Park along Michigan Avenue is famous for Cloud Gate—aka "The Bean," Crown Fountain, Jay Pritzker Pavilion, and ice-skating in the winter. As you can imagine, with so much going on, there are a countless number of dining options; let the crawl begin. . . .

1 COCHON VOLANT BRASSERIE

Ooh là là. French brasserie meets American bistro at **COCHON VOLANT** ("Flying Pig") Brasserie, located in the sophisticated Hyatt Centric The Loop. Owned and operated by WellDone Hospitality (chef Roland Liccioni and partners), the menu brings together a thoughtful marriage of French and American fare by executive chef Matt Ayala in a relaxed atmosphere. Breakfast, lunch, dinner, and weekend brunch are offered, as well as a full-service bakery and bar.

Located in the center of the financial and theater district, the restaurant is an easy-going spot to grab dinner after work or before a show. Sit back, relax, and sip on a signature or house cocktail while you leisurely browse through the menu of classic French hors d'oeuvres, salads, seafood, and more. Work your way to the Fine French Specialties section of the menu and immediately order the Truffle Pasta, a true must. It's a simple, savory dish that uses only a few ingredients: spaghetti, black truffle, Parmesan, and mixed mushrooms. Another evidently well-prepared dish is the Poulet, a 72-hour rotisseried half chicken with lemon, beef au jus, and roasted garlic.

You'll find one of the best burgers in the city right here at Cochon Volant. The Cheeseburger Royale is made with dry-aged prime beef and topped with thick-cut bacon, confit onion, American cheese, Dijonnaise, and house pickles. There is a good ratio of burger to bacon to bun.

Dessert first is the way to go on this food crawl through the loop. The Brownie à la Mode deserves stomach real estate—it can be a first course! The hot skillet comes filled with a warm, gooey chocolate brownie topped with a scoop of vanilla ice cream. Pour on the hot chocolate fudge if that isn't enough chocolate for you.

TIP

I hear chef Ayala makes his special cacio e pepe for his favorite guests. It's not on the menu, so you'll need to request but . . . shhhhhhh! Don't tell anyone else!

2 THE GAGE

Now that you've had your dessert, it's obviously time for some veggies at **THE GAGE**. The Spring Pea and Carrot Tart is a dazzling garden of vibrant vegetables sprouting out onto your plate. There is an option to add blue prawns, Amish chicken, or sea scallops to any of your salads.

Top-notch service, imaginative food, and notable drinks are what you'll find at The Gage, a modern gastropub located right on Michigan Avenue. Although it is close to Millennium Park and the Art Institute, you won't fall into the tourist trap of high-priced, below-average meals. Instead you'll find food that is tasteful without breaking the bank. Housed in a historic landmark building from the 1800s, The Gage blends old charm with new appeal.

They have a wonderful all-around menu, but I love grabbing lunch on a sunny day out on the patio and people watching. I start off by ordering the When the Livin's Easy cocktail, a refreshing mix of Grey Goose vodka, strawberries, basil, lime, and soda, and I wish every day was livin' easy. They have an expansive drink menu including ample choices of beers on draft and wine selections, classic cocktails, and seasonal cocktails. I keep going back for the Fish & Chips, which are covered in Guinness batter and fried to perfection. The Scotch Eggs are also superb, with a hard-boiled egg in the center. End the meal on a *berry* good note and get the Spring Strawberry Cheesecake with whipped mascarpone, sable, glazed berries, mint, and strawberry–passion fruit sorbet.

3

TONI PATISSERIE & CAFÉ

There's a certain *je ne sais quoi* charm to **TONI PATISSERIE & CAFÉ**. You'll find French-inspired pastries, freshly baked breads, and carefully crafted sandwiches and salads all made from scratch using premium ingredients. The warm, cozy atmosphere and friendly staff will have you daydreaming about sitting at a Parisian cafe.

Pastry chef and owner Toni Marie Cox has mastered her artistry through the years as executive pastry chef at the honorable Le Ciel Bleu in the former Mayfair Regent Hotel in Chicago as well as at the Disneyland Hotel in Paris. In 1994, she returned to Chicago, bringing a French influence to the residents of Hinsdale and then expanding with this location in the Loop.

The café menu has both European-style savory and sweet options. Savories include fan favorites like the Salade Niçoise, Croque Monsieur, Quiche Lorraine, and Ratatouille et Feta Crêpe, all served with a bountiful salad on the side. Cox's respectable background shines through in the sweet treats, which she meticulously makes with precision and care every day. The details and touches on the fruit tart are impeccable, and the layers on the White Chocolate Mousse Cake are heavenly. You can't leave a French patisserie without trying the macarons. Toni's fantastic versions are sold individually or in boxed sets. Stop in on a Thursday and get macarons for $1, all day.

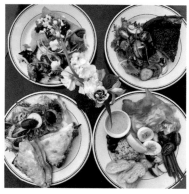

TIP

Toni Patisserie & Café, located within walking distance of Millennium Park, offers Pique-Nique boxes (one entree, one side, and one dessert). Convenient and easy for carrying to summertime picnics, concerts, and movies at the park, they are available only during the summer.

4 PRIME & PROVISIONS

In a city where we love to eat meat, there is no surprise we have a plethora of steakhouses, from tried-and-true staples to up-and-coming newbies. **PRIME & PROVISIONS**, a Dine-Amic Group concept, individuates itself from others by the quality of the beef they serve. Their mission is to serve the best meat they can source, free of antibotics and hormones, a cut above the

PRIME SOUTHSIDE COCKTAIL

2 parts The Botanist Islay Dry Gin

1 part simple syrup

1 part lemon juice

1 part egg white

7 mint leaves

rest. Their devotion to the sourcing echoes throughout the menu, with various fresh seafood, meat, and vegetable options, too. The dark wood, plush booths, and white tablecloths are expressive of an old-school supper club from the '20s, but the atmosphere here is trendy and posh.

Start off with the House-Flared Thick-Cut Bacon or Fresh Oysters. Meaty in every way, the Colossal Shrimp Cocktail is ½ pound of chilled goodness. The second-course section of the menu showcases some noticeable salads and soups like the Pickled Purple Cauliflower salad and Lump Crab & Cucumber Gazpacho, but I take a respectable pass and go straight for the steak. They serve 100 percent all-natural USDA Prime Creekstone Farms beef in various cuts, like the dry-aged porterhouse for two, bone-in rib eye, hand-cut filet mignon, and more. I asked the server for a recommendation, and he pointed me to the Dry-Aged Bone-In Kansas City Strip. He didn't steer me the wrong way. A glorious plate of meat arrived precisely sliced. I took a bite and it was blissful. The Lobster Mac & Cheese is no less divine, cheesy and creamy with big chunks of lobster. The showstopping desserts are a must. The Tableside S'mores are smokin' . . . literally. This food will fill you up and leave you content and convinced that all is good in the world. During lunch, they serve a great Dry-Aged Prime Burger with sharp Wisconsin American cheese, Dijonaise, and all the fixings. Take a midday break and check it out.

THE DEARBORN

On the corner of Dearborn and Randolph Streets you will find a welcoming ambience at an upscale eatery, **THE DEARBORN**, a perfect safe haven against the crowds and Chicago traffic. Sisters and owners Amy and Clogagh Lawless combine 40 years of hospitality experience to bring a contemporary, American tavern-style restaurant with charming service to the neighborhood. The 8,000-square-foot space is meant to evoke history, especially Chicago history, with design elements mimicking subway tiles and beams from old Chicago Transit Authority train stations.

The eclectic menu is defined as American, pulled together using locally sourced ingredients, but it includes influences from around the world. Executive chef and former *Top Chef* contestant Aaron Cuschieri wants to represent as many different cultures as possible of the melting pot that is America while staying true to the tastes of the Midwest. For example, the creamy burrata cheese is planted in the center of the plate surrounded by blossoming colors from the marinated beets, mâche, tomatoes, and swirls of sweet miso vinaigrette. Take delight in the Mediterranean flavors in The Dearborn "Meze" Plate with grape leaves, eggplant dip, white bean hummus, tabbouleh, and fattoush salad. Stuff in the pockets of the grilled pita bread and enjoy. One of the bestsellers is the Midwest Fried Chicken with maple mustard glaze, served with a house-made hot sauce and pickles. Brined for 24 hours, soaked in buttermilk, battered with secret seasonings, and fried for 15 minutes, the chicken gratifies both sweet and savory cravings. Commit to one of the desserts like the Strawberry Churros Forever with deep-fried cinnamon-spiced churros, fresh strawberries, freeze-dried strawberries, and strawberry ice cream. Dip into the Salted Dulce de Leche sauce and kiss your lips to it. Sip on the I Like It Like That cocktail, a tequila drink with fresh raspberry, citrus fruits, and sparking rosé, and stop searching. Happiness is all in your belly.

THE RIVER NORTH CRAWL

1. Take in the view at **TRAVELLE KITCHEN + BAR**, 330 N. WABASH AVE., CHICAGO, (312) 923-7705, TRAVELLECHICAGO.COM

2. Shop (and eat) 'til you drop at **LA BODEGA DEL BARRIO**, 355 N. CLARK ST., CHICAGO, BODEGAIMPORTS.COM

3. Be on the scene at **SIENA TAVERN**, 51 W. KINZIE ST., CHICAGO, (312) 595-1322, SIENATAVERN.COM

4. Pull noodles at **IMPERIAL LAMIAN**, 6 W. HUBBARD ST., CHICAGO, (312) 595-9440, IMPERIAL-LAMIAN.COM

5. Sail away to **GT FISH & OYSTER**, 531 N. WELLS ST., CHICAGO, (312) 929-3501, GTOYSTER.COM

6. Live it up **TANTA CHICAGO**, 118 W. GRAND AVE., CHICAGO, (312) 222-9700, TANTACHICAGO.COM

7. Discover the world at **ARBELLA**, 112 W. GRAND AVE., CHICAGO, (312) 846-6654, ARBELLACHICAGO.COM

8. Journey to a virtual land at **BAPTISTE & BOTTLE**, 101 E. ERIE ST., CHICAGO, (312) 667-6793, BAPTISTEANDBOTTLE.COM

9. Anchor down at **PORTSMITH**, 660 N. STATE ST., CHICAGO, (312) 202-6050, PORTSMITHCHICAGO.COM

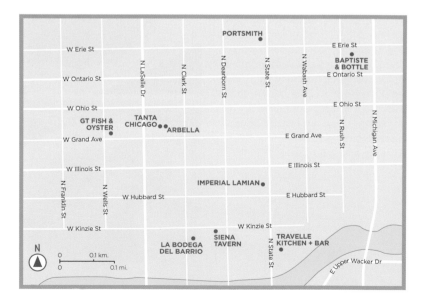

River North

River of Food Dreams

WHEN IT COMES TO RESTAURANTS, ART GALLERIES, and entertainment, River North is the heart of Downtown Chicago. Located directly north of the Loop, where the Chicago River and Michigan Avenue meet, everywhere you look are hotels, restaurants, bars, and shops. However, it was not always this way; it was once very industrial and known as "Smokey Hollow" because the smoke from factories was so thick that sunlight was often blocked. In the 1900s, the Port of Chicago relocated, straining the area's economy and earning it a reputation as Chicago's red light district. In 1964, the construction of the Marina City residential towers, corn-on-the-cob–looking buildings, just north of the river was the first step to rebirth. By the 1970s and '80s, low real estate prices attracted artists and entrepreneurs. Albert Friedman, a Chicago real estate developer, gave the area the name "River North" to help attract potential tenants.

In the past few decades, River North has redeveloped with vast high-rise buildings, nightclubs, and restaurants. Today, River North boasts one of the highest concentrations of art galleries in the United States while also offering Chicago's most vibrant nightlife—bars, dance clubs, popular restaurants, and entertainment venues. With so much to see and do, River North is a popular place for visitors to stay and for residents of all ages to call home.

1

TRAVELLE KITCHEN + BAR

TRAVELLE KITCHEN + BAR is located on the second floor of the luxurious Langham hotel with picturesque views of the river. The menu features modern interpretations of New American cuisine using sophisticated cooking techniques. The restaurant is lavish but not too formal, and the openness of the kitchen and bar makes the space look much bigger. The posh lobby is a fashion blogger's dream come true. Here's me trying to be one. OK, not so much. I think I'll stick with food.

The dishes here are all works of art—even the salad has me swooning. The Spring Panzanella Salad is a gorgeous garden of spring mix, asparagus, cucumbers, tomatoes, pumpernickel croutons, and grapefruit. For starters, order the Charred Tar, a superbly prepared tenderloin tartare with A-1 aioli, fried quail eggs, and truffle oil. The Poached Halibut with squash, matsutake ragù, and chorizo is summer on a plate and a great main option if you want to keep it light and save room for the crawl

to come. Or go all in and gratify your insatiable hunger with the Surf & Turf, a meal made for a king. This 32-ounce grilled prime tomahawk rib eye steak accompanies an herb-buttered Maine lobster served with heirloom carrots, bordelaise, and béarnaise sauce and is a great dish to share at this stop on your crawl.

The side dishes are just as noteworthy, like the Grilled Asparagus, which is prepared with vibrant radishes, microfine tarragon, parsley, and shaved truffle pecorino atop a coat of hollandaise. The Crispy Artichoke is a crowd favorite, with the different layers of flavors from the coriander, cumin, fennel seed, chile flakes, honey, pine nuts, Parmesan, orange zest, sherry vinegar puree, basil, and mint.

If you have any space left in your stomach, pastry chef Scott Green makes the most artistic desserts. His background is art and design, so the aesthetics of his dishes are just as important to him as their taste. I literally stared at the Lemon Pavlova with lemon croutons for five minutes, *oohing and aahing*, before capturing the shot.

2

LA BODEGA DEL BARRIO

"This Must Be The Place" is what you'll see on the tile floors when you enter **LA BODEGA**. It must be, because it is all over social media. Part retail and part walk-up window, La Bodega is an extension of the Mexican restaurant next door, Barrio. With the huge success of the BomboBar walk-up window at Bar Siena (check out my West Loop Dessert Crawl), DineAmic Group decided to bring a similar concept to River North.

The decor is evocative of a small market in Mexico, and the food is socially relevant and buzz-worthy. The walk-up menu is limited to coffee, churros, sundaes, and tacos, but the quality wins over the quantity. If an energizing coffee leaves a pep in your step, you will also have a smile a mile wide when you see the playful latte art. Zodiac sign? No problem. Holiday theme? Done. Your face? OK, if you really have to. I mean, they made one of Prince Harry and Meghan Markle during the royal wedding.

While you are grabbing a coffee, snatch one of the alluring churros. They come in several flavors: original, Nutella, red velvet, Fruity Pebbles, and Oreo, and they're served until they run out. Just chill with an ice cream sundae, which comes in a churro cone or cup and your choice of soft serve and three toppings.

3

SIENA TAVERN

There is always a lot of energy at **SIENA TAVERN**, parallel to the vibrant personality of executive chef and partner Fabio Viviani. Born and raised in Florence, Italy, he brings a taste of his Italian culture with a menu made from scratch in an upbeat atmosphere fit for Chicagoans.

The Coccoli is the antipasto standout—an appetizing board laden with large round crispy dough with stracchino cheese, prosciutto di Parma, and drizzles of truffle honey. The Wagyu Beef Meatball will also never disappoint, as it swims in a warm bath of roasted tomato sauce with basil and is snow-capped with bellwether ricotta. The Pizza Bar section of the menu features a variety of unique pizzas, like the Spring Vegetable, Truffle Mushroom, and Sausage and Brussels Sprouts, as well as classics like the Margherita and Burnt Pepperoni pizzas. The Burnt Pepperoni looks simple, but it tastes fierce with spicy tomato sauce and red chiles. All the pasta dishes are house-made and irresistible. They have a great selection including "Carbonara in a Jar," Short Beef Ravioli, Squid Ink Linguine, and Spaghetti with jumbo lump crab. Be *shellfish* and order the Lobster Roll for yourself. Devour the chunks of citrus-poached lobster with bacon vinaigrette, sliced tomato, and herb mayo on toasted brioche. Satisfy your sweet tooth with the Monkeybread doused with sticky caramel and finished with some candied hazelnuts and hazelnut cream.

TIP

There's a Puppy Patio available with a special menu, including a Woof-cream, dairy-free doggy dessert.

4 IMPERIAL LAMIAN

With modern furnishings and a sophisticated vibe, **IMPERIAL LAMIAN** brings refined Chinese food to the epicenter of River North with hand-pulled noodles, exceptional dim sum, memorable desserts, and Asian-inspired cocktails. Imperial Group, a well-established restaurant group based in Indonesia, has several brands and over 50 restaurants under their name. Chicago beat out New York and San Francisco as the prime location for their first US venture.

CEO and managing partner Vincent Lawrence was born and raised in Jakarta, Indonesia, and strives to change people's perspectives about Chinese food. It's not all about cheap eats in Chinatown but the dining experience as a whole.

Start off with a craft cocktail, like the Szechuan Mule with organic Prairie Cucumber Vodka, Szechuan peppercorn syrup, fresh lime juice, and ginger beer, or Smoked Rose on the Water with Hana Hou Hou Shu sparkling sake,

> *"From the ingredients we select, the cooking process and techniques, the presentation, the plates we use, to the interior design, music, as well as the service aspect, we strive to elevate the dining experience for our guests."*
>
> *Vincent Lawrence, CEO/Managing Partner*

Lillet Rosé, dill aquavit, egg white, smoked sea salt, and rose water.

The Chinese word *lā* translates to "pull" or "stretch," and *miàn* to "noodles," so you know with a name like Imperial Lamian, the hand-pulled noodles are mandatory. Peer through the open kitchen as the chefs pull, slap, and roll the noodles, which are made from scratch daily. It's a craft that takes many years to master. The end result is a uneven-edged, chewy noodle that absorbs all the flavors of the rich broth, as it does with the Brisket Lamian. The Xiao Long Bao (soup dumpling) is also handmade with precision and care. Gelatinized broth sits in the center and turns into liquid broth when steamed. The flavor bomb is juicy, savory, and hot in temperature.

The dishes here are aromatic, colorful, and tasteful, with visually appealing layers of textures. The Jasmine Tea Smoked Ribs have a subtle hint of tea flavor with a nice smokiness. The Charbroiled Seabass is cooked just right with a sweet honey glaze. The Yang Chaofan fried rice is easy on both the eyes and lips. There are several vegetarian options as well, like the Rojak Tofu, which is fried and tossed with cucumber, spicy rojak sauce, and black sesame. End your meal with the blooming Lunar Blossom; watch as the white chocolate dome melts to reveal a magnificent dessert inside.

TIP

Eat the rainbow. Try the vibrant combination Xiao Long Bao, which comes in six flavors: Shanghai (natural), spicy Szechuan (red), crab (orange), gruyère (yellow), duck (green), and truffle (black).

5

GT FISH & OYSTER

GT FISH & OYSTER is a bustling seafood-focused restaurant named after award-winning chef Giuseppe Tentori. The menu highlights both classic and contemporary dishes in a small-plate format meant for sharing. Order a few small plates to share with the group, leaving you hungry for the rest of the crawl.

The stylish nautical decor is upscale but the ambience is casual, comparable to sitting on a deck of a yacht. Grab a drink and bites at the lively bar area, opt for a seat in the dimly lit main dining area, or soak up the sun in the open patio area; wherever you choose, the mood is good.

The Oyster Po'boy Slider with kimchi and peanut is one of my favorite bites at GT Fish & Oyster. This dish is on the smaller side, so I recommend getting a few—you won't want to share! The acidity of the kimchi balances out the fried component of the dish and leaves your tongue tickling with a little spice. You *shrimply* must get the Shrimp Bruschetta. The creamy avocado puree makes a rich base on the crostini, which is layered with plump shrimp and crunchy toasted pistachio. Get reeled in by their fish options, like the Tuna Poke and Fish Tacos, a swimmingly light option.

TIP

Signature hot sauces created by the chef are available to purchase and enjoy at home.

6 TANTA CHICAGO

Take a culinary excursion to Peru at **TANTA CHICAGO,** helmed by renowned Peruvian chef Gastón Acurio, who owns several restaurants around the world.

Tanta's vibrant scene is a reliable good time. The rooftop is an absolute must during the summertime, and boozy adult beverages are unavoidable. The Pisco Sour is easy to suck down, and El Chingon with jalapeño tequila will wake you right up. The Dead Kings with Remy Martin 1738, Nardini Amaro, Cynar Argentina 70, absinthe, and lemon is also worth a try.

Peruvian food is the epitome of fusion cuisine and draws upon

"Our menu is like traveling throughout Peru, from the Pacific Ocean to playing in the desert to touring the Andes mountains, the reflection of Lake Titicaca over the Altiplano, through the amazing colors and sounds of the Amazon jungle . . . traveling, celebrating, sharing the flavors and joys of Peru and having fun with respect and gratitude to the earth."

Chef Gastón Acurio

influences from Peru's vast immigrant population, which includes people from Japan, China, Italy, and more. Expect the unexpected with exquisite dishes like the Tiraditos, which blends Japanese techniques with Peruvian ingredients. The Toreado is a skillfully plated dish of sashimi-style ahi tuna with smoky jalapeño *leche de tigre* (a citrus-based marinade), grilled corn, and torched avocado. The Niguiris Nikei resembles Japanese nigiri with combinations like the Pobre (skirt steak, quail egg, chalaca and ponzu gel) or the Criollo (scallop, Wagyu sesame beef, and polleria sauce). Get a taste of China's influence with the Chaufa Aeropuerto, Peruvian-style pork fried rice with a shrimp tortilla and spicy garlic; be sure to scoop into the crispy rice on the bottom of the hot stone bowl. Cebiche, a popular seafood dish, starts off raw and is marinated in citrus juice, which essentially "cooks" the fish and makes it safe to eat. The generous mound of fish, squid, crispy calamari, and Peruvian corn in the Cebiche Chalaco is sultry with the Peruvian rocoto pepper leche de tigre.

TIP

Chefs are always having fun and cooking up new dishes here, so make sure to check out the specials. Bursting with bold but complementary flavors, La Chuleta de Cordero y Carapulcra (grilled lamb chops with rosemary-wine reduction and sun-dried potato) was outstanding.

7 ARBELLA

If you are consumed by wanderlust or need a sensational cocktail, **ARBELLA** is THE place for you. From the out-of-this-world drink and food menu (in the form of a map) to the intriguing presentation, you'll be transported anywhere your taste buds desire without having to deal with airport security. *Amen to that!* The cocktail menu is a journey through diverse libations worldwide.

Start your exploration with Smokey the Bear, a drink poured from a smoky bear-shaped glass filled with habañero mezcal, aperitivo, lemon, and yellow Chartreuse. Next, dash over to Spain for the Spanish G&T, a classic gin and tonic with a twist. Stop in for the Frenchman Burger, a 6-ounce beef patty burger with provolone, lettuce, tomato, crispy shallots, and béarnaise. The 50 Shades of Jade takes you right into Asia with shochu, sake, violette liqueur, and Gran Classico. It states on the menu that jade "stimulates creativity and mental agility while also having a balancing and harmonizing effect." OK, I'll take five. While you're fancying Asia, try the Korean Fried Boneless Chicken. The crispy, tender chicken with a sweet-and-spicy glaze is something to write home about.

TIP

Expedite your drinking game with the A Jornada, with peppercorn-cinnamon-infused Three Sheets Spiced Rum, port wine, dragonfruit, plantain, and lemon. Arbella donates $1 to charity for each A Jornada sold every month.

8 BAPTISTE & BOTTLE

BAPTISTE & BOTTLE, perched on the 20th floor of the lavish Conrad Hotel, is a chic restaurant that boasts an impressive bourbon list, tableside bar service, and exuberant American fare by executive chef James Lintelmann. The Kampachi Crudo exhibits originality like modern art with lines, curves, and pops of bright hues: artichokes cooked *barigoule*-style, grapes, and shaved Brazilian nuts. The Burrata and Eggplant salad, composed with roasted eggplant and burrata seasoned with sumac and olive oil, exemplifies seasonality. The Roasted Amish Chicken is uncomplicated yet intricate with vivid leek puree, lightly seasoned snap peas, and Peewee potatoes. One spoonful of the Goat's Milk Cheesecake with graham crackers, strawberry, and tarragon will instantly obsess you.

The tableside cocktails are both entertaining to watch being made and enjoyable to drink. The Spanish cocktail with a side of fire will surely heat things up. When you need to escape the stresses of the real world, disappear to a virtual reality world with the #MacallanRare journey. Put on the VR glasses to learn about the Macallan story as they take you through the forests and vineyards where the drink is made while sipping on the end product.

9 PORTSMITH

Situated in the Dana Hotel, **PORTSMITH** is a seafood-focused restaurant led by chef Nate Henssler, a New Hampshire native who grew up eating a considerable amount of seafood. After working in fine dining for a decade, he wanted Portsmith to be more of an easygoing place with exceptional food. He aims for a simple approach to the preparation of the food, as he stands by the "less is more" philosophy when working with high-quality, seasonal ingredients. Don't misunderstand simplicity as lack of flavor, though. The flavors he brings forth are bright and distinctive with influences from around the world. Take the fried oysters, for example; the oyster is battered in squid-ink panko, lightly fried, and topped with a oyster basil aioli and trout roe that sits on a layer of seaweed salad. The various tastes and textures of the different components blend together to create an enlightening starter. The signature fish-and-chips is not what you would typically expect. Instead of a fried battered fish,

it's a circular piece of potatoes placed over seared Atlantic halibut with a side of malt vinegar jus and tartar sauce. How creative is that? The scallop rumaki is tender, well-prepared pieces of Georges Banks scallops and *nuoc cham* pork belly that comes elegantly plated on a bed of lemongrass-carrot puree. The whole yellowtail snapper has an Asian flair with Thai basil, shiitake mushrooms, and a special Asian XO sauce the chef created from a recipe he found in a book.

THE GOLD COAST & STREETERVILLE CRAWL

1. Appreciate the arts at **MARISOL**, 205 E. PEARSON ST., CHICAGO (312) 799-3599, MARISOLCHICAGO.COM

2. Stroll through Paris at **PETIT MARGEAUX** and **MARGEAUX BRASSERIE**, 11 E. WALTON ST., CHICAGO (312) 625-1324, MICHAELMINA.NET/ RESTAURANTS/CHICAGO/

3. Keep it reel at **HUGO'S FROG BAR & FISH HOUSE**, 1024 N. RUSH ST., CHICAGO, (312) 640-0999, HUGOSFROGBAR.COM

4. Feast at **GIBSONS BAR & STEAKHOUSE**, 1028 N. RUSH ST., CHICAGO, (312) 266-8999, GIBSONSSTEAKHOUSE.COM

5. See and be seen at **MAPLE & ASH**, 8 W. MAPLE ST., CHICAGO, (312) 944-8888, MAPLEANDASH.COM

6. Country club it up at **SOMERSET**, 1112 N. STATE ST., CHICAGO, (312) 586-2150, SOMERSETCHICAGO.COM

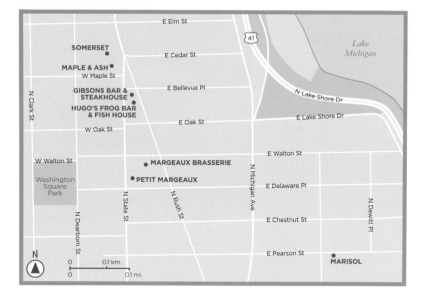

Gold Coast & Streeterville

Toast to the Coast

GOLD COAST AND STREETERVILLE are two of Chicago's wealthiest neighborhoods located adjacent to the Magnificent Mile. Named for the expensive stretch of lakefront property it sits on—between Oak Street and North Avenue Beaches—the Gold Coast is known for its stately homes on quiet tree-lined streets. It is well-known for high-end shopping at the boutiques on Oak Street as well as evenings on famed Rush Street, which has long been, and still is, known for its vibrant nightlife and hot spots.

Neighboring Streeterville, which many say is part of Gold Coast, also sits on prime lakefront property—between Navy Pier and Oak Street Beach. Streeterville is named after George Wellington Streeter, who claimed he stranded his boat on a sandbar in the late 1800s and created the land. Sitting between Lake Michigan and the Magnificent Mile of Michigan Avenue, Streeterville is home to many popular tourist attractions—875 North Michigan Avenue (the skyscraper formerly known as John Hancock Center), the historic Drake Hotel, the Museum of Contemporary Art, Navy Pier and Chicago Children's Museum, Ohio Street Beach, and much more. With numerous hotels in Gold Coast and Streeterville, the area is surrounded by a variety of restaurants, which I think is the best part!

1

MARISOL

MARISOL, located at the Museum of Contemporary Art, will heighten your senses with vibrant art and design by British artist Chris Ofili and imaginative dishes by the outstanding chef Jason Hammel (chef-owner of Lula Cafe in Logan Square). Chef de cuisine Sarah Rinkavage works together with Hammel to create a menu where art is food and food is art, inspired by the French-Venezuelan sculptor Marisol Escobar. Her piece *Six Women* was the first artwork acquired for the museum.

Based on available seasonal ingredients, the menu is ever-changing but consistently bright and balanced. Rinkavage likes to keep the presentation clean and minimalistic, using monotone colors to play off the lively colors of the museum's look and feel. Meal sharing is the focus, and simplicity is the foundation. Tender pieces of sliced chilled octopus drizzled in citrus oil arrive with a side of addictive saffron-spiced chips. Next came the burrata with fennel, bay leaf, and green almonds with a side of thick-cut bread. Don't pass over the Sunflower Hummus served alongside a plate of flaxseed crackers; with artichokes, oregano, and hints of spice, it's not your average hummus. The Green Circle Roasted Half Chicken pairs well with potatoes, green garlic, and chamomile.

2 PETIT MARGEAUX AND MARGEAUX BRASSERIE

The Waldorf Astoria is undeniably one of most extravagant hotels in Chicago, with its immaculate courtyard and grandiose ambience. These two dining establishments are no less awe-inspiring with their 1920s Paris decor. James Beard award–winning chef and restaurateur Michael Mina brings French

cuisine with a Midwestern flair to the Gold Coast at **PETIT MARGEAUX** and **MARGEAUX BRASSERIE**.

Petit Margeaux, located in the lobby of the Waldorf Astoria, brings a little piece of Parisian charm to Chicago. The menu features various coffees, teas, pastries, and light bites.

I am immediately distracted by the perfectly lined-up pastries in the display case, and my eyes zoom in on the cylinder-shaped, shiny pink dessert—a Strawberry Cheesecake, a capsule of pure delight. The large colorful macarons are light, airy, and absolutely satisfactory. Pastry chef Ashley Torto's techniques shine through in the layers of the buttery croissants. The tender, moist Blueberry Scones are flecked with a liberal serving of blueberries drizzled with a light glaze.

The menu at Margeaux Brasserie is reminiscent of a Parisian brasserie with French classics like escargot, onion soup, and frog legs made with exceptional locally sourced ingredients. Since I can't hop on a plane to Paris any time I want (have you tried traveling with a toddler?), I'm happy there is a chic French option right in my hometown, especially with a *merveilleux* brunch.

Generous amounts of blueberries and a spoonful of lemon curd cover the thick piece of Margeaux French Toast. For savories, the Croque Madame is exquisite with the sunny-side up egg and gruyère fondue poured on top; the slight saltiness of the ham and sweetness of the marmalade balance

the whole dish. Opt for the Smoked Salmon Benedict with a flaky, buttery croissant, which melts in your mouth, and a rich béarnaise sauce. Keep it simple with the rotating fluffy quiche, which is also available at Petit Margeaux.

Signature dishes like the Daily Crudo and Hand-Ground Steak Tartare are available on both the dinner and brunch menus.

3 HUGO'S FROG BAR & FISH HOUSE

HUGO'S FROG BAR & FISH HOUSE is a respectable seafood restaurant that has been around since 1997. Partners Hugo Ralli and Steve Lombardo opened this first location next door to their extremely popular steakhouse, Gibsons Bar & Steakhouse. Hugo's name comes from Ralli's grandfather, whose nickname was Frog. They have two other Illinois locations in Naperville and Des Plaines, as well as one in Philadelphia.

You won't find ultra-trendy food here, but you will find classic, well-prepared dishes using top-notch ingredients. The portions are huge, so come hungry and ready to share. There is a little bit of everything on the menu, from salads to burgers to steaks to their signature frog legs, but the seafood offerings are what really shine on the menu. Fresh oysters, slices of seared sesame tuna, ginormous shrimp, and Alaskan king crab bites magnificently showcase their cold raw selections. The Shrimp Dejonghe comes with succulent pieces of shrimp laid on a bed of garlicy wine sauce and topped with bread crumbs. For a fantastic fish option, try the Chilean

Sea Bass, beautifully prepared with a miso glaze and hon-shimeji mushrooms and peas.

A chocolate lover's dream, the famously monstrous (literally, the size of your face) Chocolate Mousse Pie is layered with chocolate fudge cake, chocolate mousse, chocolate frosting, and white and milk chocolate shavings.

TIP

Hugo's shares a kitchen with its sister restaurant, Gibsons Bar & Steakhouse, so you can order a nice juicy steak to pair with your seafood. Best of both worlds, the Steak & Cake is a wonderful surf-and-turf option featuring a 10-ounce filet and a jumbo lump crab cake with hot pink mayonnaise.

4

GIBSONS BAR & STEAKHOUSE

Opened in 1989, **GIBSONS BAR & STEAKHOUSE** is an iconic restaurant for premium meats and excellent service in a highly sociable environment. Pictures of celebrities who have dined there adorn the walls. Conveniently located in the exclusive Gold Coast neighborhood, it is great for power business lunches, happy hour, and special occasions.

Balance your meat consumption with a delightful seafood appetizer like the Crabmeat Avocado or Shrimp Cocktail—true classics. Make sure to wash it down with an old-school cocktail like a Dirty Martini. Gibsons proudly serves USDA Gibsons Prime Angus beef, which comes from a sustainable farm and is aged for 40 days to perfection. They are the first restaurant group in the United States to be awarded their own certification. Impressive! The signature W.R.'s Chicago Cut is a tremendous 22-ounce bone-in rib eye in which all carnivores will rejoice. Seasonal vegetables or Double Baked Potato? Double baked potato (of course!) because

it still counts as a vegetable, right? Local favorites include Prime Rib French Dip, Baby Back Ribs, Whole-Spit Roasted Chicken, and Lamb Chops. The Van Well Family Farm Lamb Chops come in three luscious pieces paired with minty green gelatin. Go all out and get the monumental Carrot Cake. You can work out your biceps lifting that thing up—exactly the type of workout I like.

MAPLE & ASH

MAPLE & ASH is an extravagant Gold Coast steakhouse that exudes luxury. The massive, dimly lit restaurant is lavishly decorated with illuminating candles, elongated candelabras, flowy sheer drapes, and a dramatic looping chandelier. Take it all in and don't be intimidated by the white tablecloths and upscale vibe. The staff is unpretentious and the cuisine approachable.

Enjoy a traditional steak dinner with prime cuts of meat and classic sides or opt for a completely different experience with wood-fired and fire-roasted dishes curated by two Michelin-star chef Danny Grant. Either way, there is always a little humor added. Get the "I Don't Give a F*@k," a chef's choice option for $145. With the neighborhood deemed the "Viagra Triangle," the menu features sauces titled Arm Candy and uses terms like

Semi-Pro and Baller to denote portion sizes of the Seafood Tower. LOL. Speaking of Seafood Tower, an assortment of oysters, scallops, Maine lobster, Manila clams, blue prawn, and Alaskan king crab are fire-roasted in the hearth and bathed in garlic butter and chile oil. Squeeze the lemon juice to kick up the flavors. Another great seafood option is the Mediterranean Branzino, grilled and served over a bed of shaved fennel, capers, and preserved lemon. They also have an entree section where they feature pork, chicken, and house-made pastas.

But we all know you came for the meat, so let's get right to it. There are lots of options to choose from, including Bone-In Rib Eye, Cowgirl, Filet, New York Strip, Pork Chop, Tomahawk, and Rack of Lamb. Treat yourself to the Spinalis Steak, a super-tender, extra-marbled meat surrounding the rib eye. Pair it with one of the market sides like the Baked & Loaded. Layers of braised short rib, creamy potato puree, sour cream, and melty cheese are capped with crispy bacon and fried onions to form a big mound of goodness. Pour the jus for the finishing touch.

For a more casual vibe, check out Maple & Ash's patio area called 8 Bar. It's perfect for cocktails, light bites, late night, weekend brunch, and people watching!

6

SOMERSET

SOMERSET serves seasonal American cuisine with a contemporary country club feel. It is situated on the main floor of Viceroy Chicago, a space formerly occupied by the historic Cedar Hotel. The splashy atmosphere has a 1960s yacht club mood, with navy blue banquettes, soaring high ceilings, and custom wood flooring. When the Boka Restaurant Group (Kevin Boehm and Rob Katz) opens a restaurant, one can't expect anything less than spectacular, especially with chef Lee Wolen helming the kitchen. Wolen is also the executive chef–partner of the acclaimed Boka, the group's first restaurant.

Wolen takes a similar approach as he does at Boka, but here it's approachable and accessible. He focuses on seasonal ingredients

while thoughtfully highlighting the classic flavors, describing it as "food people like to eat." They are open for breakfast, lunch, and dinner every day and for brunch on the weekends. Expect to find a version of the Vegetarian Flatbread with ingredients like oyster mushrooms and caramelized onions. Rotating pastas and salads are featured, including a Beet Salad with strawberries and granola. Seared Tuna or Seared Halibut swim in beautiful, bright flavors and colors. Meat dishes include Roasted Beef Short Ribs, Aged Roasted Duck, Somerset Cheeseburger, and Roasted Lamb Loin & Sausage with spring peas, grains, and feta, to name a few. Desserts are a must! Choose Pavlova, Chocolate Mousse, Buckwheat Carrot Cake, or my favorite, Somerset Sundae. Every day should be sundae. There is also a happening bar, so grab a cocktail and stay awhile.

THE WEST TOWN CRAWL

1. Share a sea of small plates at **BAR BISCAY**, 1450 W. CHICAGO AVE., CHICAGO, (312) 455-8900, BARBISCAY.COM

2. Chair dance your meal away at **BEATNIK**, 1604 W. CHICAGO AVE., CHICAGO, (312) 929-4945, BEATNIKCHICAGO.COM

3. Just brew it at **FORBIDDEN ROOT RESTAURANT & BREWERY**, 1746 W. CHICAGO AVE., CHICAGO, (312) 929-2202, FORBIDDENROOT.COM

4. Life is what you bake it at **WEST TOWN BAKERY & DINER**, 1916 W. CHICAGO AVE., CHICAGO, (773) 904-1414, WESTTOWNBAKERY.COM

5. Brunch like you mean it at **WHISK**, 2018 W. CHICAGO AVE., CHICAGO, (773) 252-9060, WHISKCHICAGO.COM

6. Wine all the time at **CAFÉ MARIE-JEANNE**, 1001 N. CALIFORNIA AVE., (773) 904-7660, CAFE-MARIE-JEANNE.COM

7. Walk on the wild side at **FRONTIER**, 1072 N. MILWAUKEE AVE., (773) 772-4322, THEFRONTIERCHICAGO.COM

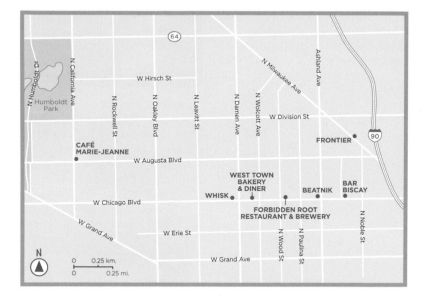

West Town

Chicago's Wild, Wild West

WEST TOWN IS AN UNTAPPED COMMUNITY located northwest of the Loop—untapped in that it is still relatively free of big-box establishments, which can often take away uniqueness and authenticity. Don't get me wrong, I enjoy my Starbucks Iced Skinny Caramel Macchiato as much as the next gal, but variety is the spice of life. Other neighborhoods associated with West Town are Humboldt Park, Noble Square, Ukrainian Village, and, of course, West Town.

As with most communities in Chicago, West Town is a diverse cross-section of nationalities. Once the heart of the Polish downtown, the Mexican, Puerto Rican, and Ukrainian cultures are also prevalent today. Chicago Avenue serves as the main corridor and has seen wonderful changeover in storefronts, with new restaurants, bars, and shops opening next to older established businesses—think local fashion boutiques, antiques, vintage accessories, coffee shops, and more. Add in the numerous art galleries, churches, museums, music venues, and theaters, and West Town is worth a visit.

1

BAR BISCAY

Biscay is a Spanish province south of Bay of Biscay in the Basque country. **BAR BISCAY** in West Town is a Spanish brasserie with French influences serving *mano a boca* ("hand to mouth," or small bites) as well as large plates in a relaxed *pinxto* (snack or tapas) bar setting. The lively atmosphere with neon lights and house-party music is the concept of owners Sari Zernich Worsham and Scott Worsham, along with partner Joe Campagna.

Chef Johnny Anderes (formerly of Honey's) commands the kitchen, where simplicity is at the core with a less-is-more philosophy. Seasonal vegetables dishes are a big highlight on the menu. Think slender charred carrots on lentil purée and *labneh* spiced with Espelette chile pepper, or the radishes with watercress tossed in lardon vinaigrette. The grilled asparagus spears with romesco sauce are effortless and brilliant. Get bready for the toast offerings. There are many to choose from. Strawberries and Queixo Tetilla cheese, duck rillette and green onions, and octopus and garlic butter—whatever floats your toast. "From the Sea" choices include oysters, smoked sardines, and littleneck clams, while cheeses and meats are presented "From the Land." Steaks, chops, duck, and whole fish come in large plate formats in addition to the *poussin* (small chicken) with strawberry and fava beans. Anchor down and eat up.

BEATNIK

BEATNIK, a Boho-chic restaurant inspired by the 1950s, is all-around luxurious and one of the most aesthetically pleasing restaurants in Chicago. The 6,000-square-foot space is illuminated with extravagant hanging chandeliers salvaged from the ballroom of the historic Century Plaza Hotel in Los Angeles and, in the center of the dining room, a colossal (40 foot wide by 10 foot high) carved teak facade imported from Bali. No detail is left untouched, from restored cast-iron streetlights hanging from the bar to the Parisian patisserie counter to the hand-knotted rugs from the Middle East. Founder Daniel Alonso and his partners handpicked each element to bring truly out-of-this-world pieces with symbolism and significance.

Chef Marcos Campos started his culinary journey at the young age of 15, when he took over his father's butcher shop in Valencia, Spain, where he grew up. He spent most of his career in Spain, including a stint at

Michelin-star Las Rejas under famed chef Manolo de la Osa. Campos joined Bonhomme Hospitality Group in 2012 and uses his experience to create exotic flavors, drawing influences from around the world, including Greece, India, Japan, and Morocco. The menu is mainly focused on meze (small plates) such as the Smoked Baba Ghanoush, a dazzling spread of tahini yogurt drizzled with fig balsamic vinegar and spiced with black garlic and za'atar.

Even the veggies are decked out, as in the case of the Charred Broccolini with *nuoc cham* (Vietnamese sweet and sour sauce), sunflower hummus, pomegranate seeds, and puffed rice. The Curry Meatballs pop off the plate, with vibrant hues from the vivid green avocado hummus and dollops of an orangish puree made with sun-dried tomatoes and harissa. Specks of chia seeds sprinkle the top of thick-cut chunks of Hamachi Crudo with chopped apples surrounded by a pool of green gazpacho. Menu items listed under "Feast" are great for sharing, with options including a 45-ounce aged bone-in rib eye, wild lobster, and whole fish dressed with green harissa, Mediterranean *amba*, pickled red onions, and herb salad. By the way, you will be chair dancing to the beats of the DJ mixing reggae, Middle Eastern classic rock, and Brazilian soul.

Cocktails and drinks are a big focus here. Enjoy boozy Freezin' My Nuts Off slushies or A Friend from Miami (red bell pepper three ways, blanco tequila, agave, lime, and soda) and Mámù Vida (mezcal, chipotle, Szechuan peppercorns, honey, lemon, *sal de gusano*) shaken and stirred mixtures. Kenny's Redemption Sour is a popular pisco sour drink with kaffir lime leaves, lemongrass, lemon, lime, and aquafaba.

3 FORBIDDEN ROOT

Part restaurant, part brewery, **FORBIDDEN ROOT** is Chicago's premiere spot for fine botanic beers, with a menu loaded with comfort foods crafted around complementing brews. Founder and rootmaster Robert Finkel is passionate about craft brewing, experimenting with natural ingredients, and getting to the root of pure flavors and aromas. He is dedicated to the process, research, techniques, and innovation in order to formulate distinctive beers you can't find anywhere else. It is a true art form that utilizes flowers, roots, and herbs. Essence of wild strawberries and basil resurrect in the Strawberry Basil Hefeweizen, German-style wheat ale, while the Toro Triple, a

New England–style IPA, has a honey sweetness component from the cantaloupe. Beers are mixed into cocktails, as is the case with the Rake-olo, made with Forbidden Root Piccolo pale ale.

Brew-tiful food pairings, prepared by chef Dan Weiland are pleasant twists on familiar foods. Chicagoans love their giardiniera, and the Fried Giardiniere with oregano-chipotle salt and ranch dressing has me hooked. Snack on the spicy, spreadable 'nduja Sausage studded with pickled mustard seeds and spread bountifully over the grilled honey toast. The Malted Lamb Ribs are served on the bone, glazed with tamarind sorghum, and intensified with herbs and pickled Fresno peppers. Now, can we talk about the burger for a minute? It's probably one of the most underrated burgers in the city. You need this in your life ASAP. A thick patty with giardiniera mayo, aged cheddar, onions, and bread-and-butter pickles come between a toasted brioche bun. Cut into the massive Milk Brined Pork Schnitzel Sandwich to uncover the pickled-beet mayo and slaw.

TIP

32- and 64-ounce growlers are available for purchase. They are recyclable and dishwasher-safe. And 100 percent of Forbidden Root's nonconsumable merchandise profits, including the growler container, go to charity.

4   WEST TOWN BAKERY & DINER

WEST TOWN BAKERY & DINER is a full-service bakery and restaurant serving breakfast and lunch in a funky atmosphere with graffiti walls and retro diner vibes. They are committed to being a sustainable bakery in all aspects of their business. From the food to the packaging to the lighting, everything is consciously thought out with the environment in mind. They are also dedicated to feeding everyone. Whether you have health conditions or special requests, including nut-, soy-, gluten-, and dairy-free, they try their best to accommodate your needs.

I casually stroll through the bakery section, but my eyes are intensely rolling up and down the display cases of colorful doughnuts, croissants, chocolates, and pastries. Executive pastry chef Chris "Tex" Teixeira aims not only to make the pastries and chocolates taste good but also look good. Teixeira combines two of his favorite things, cereal and croissants, for the ultimate breakfast on the go. The Cereal Bowl Croissants are filled with cereal-infused whipped cream and topped with vanilla or chocolate glaze. As Rappin' Barney would say, you will "love Fruity Pebbles in a major way." I can get behind *hole* foods like their doughnuts. The chocolate glazed is sprinkled with rainbow specks while the Homer doughnut has a pretty *D'OH*-pe, radiant pink glaze! *Doughnut* leave without the cream cheese–frosted red velvet, coffee-flavored Dark Matter, or the glazed, doughy Chris P Cream. Life is short, have a ball: cakeball, that is! Made from scraps of custom cakes, these rich, round bites come in a multitude of flavors, including red velvet, chocolate chip, chocolate sprinkle, vanilla sprinkle, french toast, chocolate peanut, lemon almond, and triple chocolate. You'll be straight up ballin'. I just wanna have *abs*olutely more chocolate. Treat yourself to the Caramelized Rice Treats, Sammy's Mints, and Turtles because why give up on chocolate? You're no quitter.

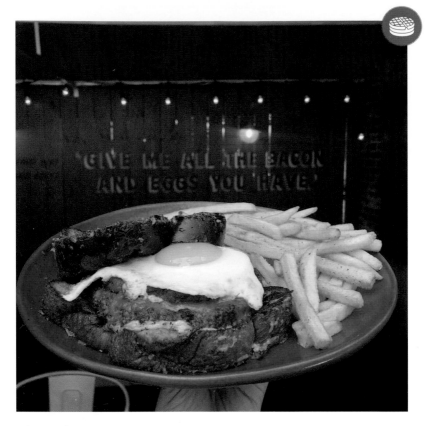

WHISK

Chefs-owners Rick and David Rodriguez serve "brunch by day, burgers by night" plus a whole lot of Ron Swanson all day, everyday. The two brothers combine their love for burgers (Rick) and pancakes + *Parks and Recreation* (David) for an entertaining brunch spot known as **WHISK**. You can't help but notice the portraits of Ron Swanson, painted by local artists, covering the walls. All I can think is "there has never been a sadness that can't be cured by breakfast food." Whatever vibe they are channeling, it is working. I'm feeling it.

The brunch menu features all the American breakfast classics with a Mexican spin, including huevos rancheros, chilaquiles, and chorizo omelette. Save room for the "Sweet" section. You will know why later. Remaining true to Swanson's style, there's bacon and eggs as well as biscuits and gravy. Two cheery sunny-side up eggs sit atop buttery biscuits dripping with white sausage gravy and served with house potatoes. And, because you can't have enough biscuits and gravy, chef Rick's version is topped with fried chicken breast, his take on a "Benedict." Give your taste buds a kick with the Buffalo Chicken Hash, a mass of house potatoes and buffalo chicken with chunks of avocado, bacon, tomato, and lettuce. The mountain of food is capped with two poached eggs and finished with ranch dressing. David's Special has a lot of grit—cheesy grits, that is, with sautéed garlic shrimp, bacon, mushrooms, and scallions in a wine-and-cream sauce. OK, remember how I told you to save room? Don't drool on this book when I tell you they have Pumpkin Cinnamon Roll Pancakes, Oreo Raspberry Pancakes, Snickers Stuffed French Toast, and more. (Wait, did you just drool?) Moving on, order the Reese's Pancakes: white chocolate, milk chocolate, Reese's chocolate pieces, and chocolate mascarpone. I'm wasted on chocolate and don't ever want to sober up.

TIP

Burgers are available starting at 11 a.m. The House Burger and Old Time Burger can be made breakfast-style. Swap out the bun for french toast and the bacon for sausage.

6

CAFÉ MARIE-JEANNE

Occupying the corner of California Avenue and Augusta Boulevard sits a homey spot, **CAFÉ MARIE-JEANNE**, serving a French-influenced menu for breakfast, lunch, and dinner. Marie-Jeanne is a large wine bottle that holds about three times the standard amount and is used in the establishment's name to signify gathering, sharing, and socializing. Husband-and-wife duo Michael Simmons and Val Szafranski live in the neighborhood and stay true to the casual, upbeat vibe of Humboldt Park. They wanted a place in the area where people can come and have a well-prepared meal paired with good wine. Stop and drink the rosé.

Simmons (formerly of Lula Cafe and Rootstock) uses straightforward French-style cooking influenced by the things he likes to eat. He centers on using premium in-season ingredients to highlight bright, natural flavors. The Market Veggies and Onion Dip is a blooming bouquet of fresh vegetables sprouting out of a bowl of onion dip. Enjoy French classics like the steak tartare served with a crusty, full loaf of bread. Half or full portions can be order of the smoked chicken. Cut in big chunks, the skin is crispy, with hints of woodiness and herbs. The quail eggs with ramp mayo, bread crumbs, and edible flowers are both unique and stunning. Breakfast is the most important meal of the day, so fuel up with à la carte items such as fruit, toast, and meats, or opt for a sweet or savory pastry.

Try the build-your-own breakfast sandwich. Pick two items from various options as simple as bacon or as unusual as sautéed calf brains. It also includes one egg, any style, and cheese on country wheat or English muffin. Bottarga, steelhead roe, caviar, or searod foie gras are optional for an additional cost. Switch out the bread for any biscuit or croissant for $3.

7 FRONTIER

Take a journey to the wild, wild, west (town) to **FRONTIER**, where they say, "Nature dictates what's on the menu." Set in a rustic modern-day lodge and rooted in the traditions of the pioneers of the American West, Frontier specializes in comfort food and whole animal service using a farm-to-table approach. The atmosphere is designed around communal dining with a spirited beer garden. Executive chef Brian Jupiter, a New Orleans native, blends his Southern background, culinary training, and hunter-gatherer approach to create a one-of-a-kind experience with unique offerings like alligator, water buffalo, and antelope. Lucky for you, no hunting gear is needed on your end.

To share, the chargrilled oysters are shucking tasty with Creole butter, bread crumbs, Parmesan, and chives. Shuck, slurp, repeat. Oh, *kale* yeah! The kale salad has the texture of coleslaw with crunchy bites of red cabbage,

apples, dates, and chives, all tossed in a tangy sherry vinaigrette. It's piled in a perfect cylinder shape and embellished with goat cheese and gooseberries. Hold up, this mama needs a cocktail, and so do you. The Verditarita deserves the limelight with tequila, lime, and house-made verdita (cilantro, mint, jalapeño, and pineapple juice). If you'd prefer a vodka drink, the Pamplemousse is a fruity mixture with grapefruit, lemon, and delicate elderflower. In a city filled with burgers, it is always nice to see a different version, and the lamb burger with cucumber-dill yogurt, provolone, harissa aioli, and arugula is an excellent alternative. The melt-in-your-mouth Wagyu sirloin is free of hormones and antibotics, and it's seasoned with smoked peppercorns and crested with blue cheese butter. Let's talk more cheese. The 5 Cheese Mac is a Frontier classic, with twisty rotini and five different kinds of cheese. All the flavors are locked in the spirals, making each and every bite super cheesy.

WHOLE ANIMAL SERVICE INCLUDES:

Animal of choice, such as alligator, goat, lamb, and more are available. Prices vary.

Coordinated sides are included based on the animal.

Optional shots for the table, large format cocktails, and desserts are available for an additional charge.

THE WICKER PARK & BUCKTOWN CRAWL

1. Taste the cravings at **MOTT STREET**, 1401 N. ASHLAND AVE., CHICAGO, (773) 687-9977, MOTTSTREETCHICAGO.COM

2. Tex-Mex it up at **DOVE'S LUNCHEONETTE**, 1545 N. DAMEN AVE., CHICAGO, (773) 645-4060, DOVESCHICAGO.COM

3. Hunker down at **PUBLICAN ANKER**, 1576 N. MILWAUKEE AVE., CHICAGO, (773) 904-1121, PUBLICANANKER.COM

4. Feed your heart and soul at **MINDY'S HOTCHOCOLATE**, 1747 N. DAMEN AVE., CHICAGO, (773) 489-1747, HOTCHOCOLATECHICAGO.COM

5. Feel the nostalgia at **MARGIE'S CANDIES**, 1960 N. WESTERN AVE., CHICAGO, (773) 384-1035, MARGIESFINECANDIES.COM

6. Transport yourself to Paris at **LE BOUCHON**, 1958 N. DAMEN AVE., (773) 862-6600, LEBOUCHONOFCHICAGO.COM

7. Satiate your hunger at **THE BRISTOL**, 2152 N. DAMEN AVE., (773) 862-5555, THEBRISTOLCHICAGO.COM

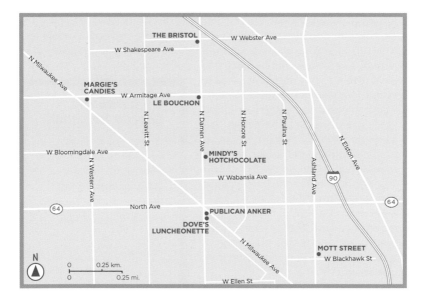

Wicker Park & Bucktown

West Side Food Story

WICKER PARK AND BUCKTOWN ARE ADJACENT NEIGHBORHOODS located northwest of the Loop. These artsy, hip neighborhoods come together at Six Corners—the intersection of North, Damen, and Milwaukee Avenues; sprawling out from there you will find a treasure trove of shopping, good eats, coffee, desserts, and craft cocktails. From major retail-chain fashion to small boutiques, thrift shops, and vintage stores, the once hipster area has become trendy with an edge. When the sun goes down, you can find whatever nightlife you desire—craft cocktails, mixology lounge, sports bars, music venues, microbreweries, and more.

Historically home to Polish, German, Puerto Rican, and other Latino immigrants, Wicker Park and Bucktown are now popular with and home to many young professionals, due to the proximity to the Loop and public transportation. Residents and guests alike also enjoy easy access to the 606—the former elevated train line converted to a public trail system. Along the 2.7-mile trail that runs through Wicker Park, Bucktown, Humboldt Park, and Logan Square, you can see the residential diversity of older single-family homes, modern condo and apartment buildings, and converted industrial loft spaces.

1

MOTT STREET

MOTT STREET is the brainchild of partners chef Edward Kim, Jenny Kim, Vicki Kim, and Nate Chung and highlights globally inspired Asian fare. The name is a tribute to New York City's Mott Street, the "main street" in Chinatown, as well as a play on the Korean word *mott*, meaning "taste." The team opened Mott Street in 2013, a time when the area was still underdeveloped, but through their commitment, they soon turned the rough corner of Ashland Avenue and Blackhawk Street into a shining bright light, even getting recognition from the alderman. Chef Kim shares that his proudest moments aren't the numerous accolades but their growth and evolution with the neighborhood; instilling a sense of professionalism and helping fight crime are their real honored accomplishments.

Edward Kim takes his classically trained background, his Korean roots, and the cravings of his team to create dishes prepared with thoughtfulness fueled by connection that will ignite fond memories. You will find communal tables and family-style dishes with an eclectic bar program. Start off with the pan-seared oyster mushrooms immersed in miso butter and garnished with thyme. The stuffed cabbage is Polish *golabki* meets Korean kimchi. The flavors are distinctively Korean—kimchi, pork butt, and sticky rice—with remnants of a dish from a Polish grandma's kitchen, combined using refined techniques. Eat noods and get the Mentaiko Udon, my favorite dish on the menu. Grab your chopsticks and twirl in the kimchi nage (kimchi juice, chicken stock, and butter) with the thick, chewy noodles. The spicy marinated cod roe, dancing bonita flakes, and seasoned nori provide a subtle taste of the sea. Get hoppin' on the Rabbit Laap, a modern take on a celebratory Laotian dish with sticky rice, quinoa, buckwheat, flax, hemp, toasted rice, and cacao nibs. Since friends don't let friends go thirsty, let's talk about some of the seasonal cocktails. From turmeric-infused honey to apple-poblano-sage mixtures, the drinks are always interesting. The Ruffled Feathers cocktail will make you think of spring picking with its strawberry syrup and muddled strawberries. Calm your nerves with the Folk Remedy, a bourbon drink with honey-chamomile syrup and ginseng.

Check out their sister restaurant, Mini Mott, in Logan Square, where they serve one of the best burgers in the city. The double chuck patty burger is piled high with sweet potato shoestrings, pickled jalapeños, dill pickles, and American cheese. It can get kinda messy, but you won't care.

DOVE'S LUNCHEONETTE

Located near the Damen "L" stop on the Blue Line, you'll find a diner with retro vibes and an all-day breakfast menu. **DOVE'S LUNCHEONETTE** is Wicker Park's go-to spot for Southern-inspired Mexican fare and mezcal cocktails. It is a no-judgment type of place where anyone can walk in for a great meal and good conversations while listening to the blues. The space seats around 40 on old-school diner counters and stools. This One Off Hospitality concept was named after Nelson Algren's *A Walk on the Wild Side*, a novel set during the Depression about a man named Dove Linkhorn.

In his prior life, chef de cuisine Tom Carlin lived and worked in Texas, where he honed his techniques and the flavors of Southern cuisine. He draws upon those experiences as well as his butchery skills from his time at Publican Quality Meats to create distinctive southern Tex-Mex offerings. The menu is broken out by small plates, plates, ceviche, sides, and daily specials. The seafood "Back to Life Cocktail" will bring you back to life with the zest from the lime and a little kick from the habañeros: A vintage-inspired fountain shoppe glass is overflowing with chunks of Dungeness crab, squid, and shrimp, lightly marinated in citrus juices and tossed with tomatoes, habañero, avocado, and cilantro. The Chicken Fried Chicken, dripping in chorizo verde gravy with bright green sweet peas and fragrant pearl onions is the epitome of comfort food. Carlin takes the barbecue right out of Texas and puts it into the Burnt Ends Hash: Brisket burnt ends, crispy potatoes, and poblano peppers are tossed with a rich aioli and blanketed with two sunny-side up eggs. Pile it up on the thick-cut Texas toast. A bowl of satisfaction comes in the shape of the Copa de Puerco, a

slow-roasted pork shoulder combined with creamed hominy and collard greens. It's topped off with a fried egg and garnished with parsley and crispy bits. Enhance your flavorsome bowl of Pozole Rojo, slow-braised pork shoulder in a guajillo chile broth, with cabbage, avocado, radish, and cilantro, and squeeze the lime on top to add a little citrus tang.

They have a wide selection of tequila and mezcal as well a few selections of beer and wine. Have you ever had a Mexican Squirt soda? The Cantarito cocktail has Lunazul Blanco, orange and grapefruit juices, salt, and Mexican Squirt.

3 PUBLICAN ANKER

PUBLICAN ANKER is the sister restaurant of the ever popular The Publican in the West Loop, but different. Different in the way it caters to the low-pressure vibe of Wicker Park, playing homage to the early 20th-century saloons that once existed in the neighborhood. You will still see familiar touches from The Publican, including the recognizable orb lights. It is an easy-going spot to hunker down for beers and upscale pub food.

The seasonal menu is straightforward with Oysters, Snacks, Vegetables, Burgers, Charcoal & Wood Grilled, and daily Chalkboard Specials, with a wide selection of craft beers and cocktails. Chef de cuisine A. J. Walker, a reputable member of the One Off Hospitality family, has an uncomplicated approach to food and focuses on the main ingredients. Get raw with the freshly shucked oysters from both the East and West Coasts, or order the grilled oysters drenched in yuzu kosho butter. Wash it all down with a Hamm on Rye, a can of Hamm's beer with a shot of Rittenhouse Rye. If you fancy a cocktail, the Six Corner Shuffle Cocktail with Letherbee gin and Apologue Celery Root Herbal Liqueur will calm your nerves after all the hustle and bustle of city life. Fried smelt with dill pickle mayo was a pleasant twist on a normally drab salad. Encased Swordfish Sausage was well-prepared with citrusy tangerine salsa verde and fennel. The Pub Burger is a nice, solid burger with a simple presentation of caramelized onions, American cheese, and creamy McDreamy special sauce.

4 MINDY'S HOTCHOCOLATE

Chef-owner Mindy Segal is a James Beard and Jean Banchet Award–swinning pastry chef, and undoubtedly the Queen Bee of desserts in Chicago. Segal's restaurant **HOTCHOCOLATE** is a quintessential Chicago spot that has been serving sugar devotees and ravenous diners in Bucktown since 2005. Yes, there is hot chocolate. And, yes, it's absolutely divine! But it's more than just hot chocolate and desserts. Segal is passionate about feeding people with heart and soul. Her hands-on approach and dedication to her craft are evident in the end products. She's also a big supporter of small businesses, local sourcing, and cooking from scratch with natural ingredients.

HotChocolate offers lunch, dinner, fabulous desserts, and weekend brunch. Go *cocoa* over the chocolate drinks, available hot or iced, served with house-made marshmallows. Options include medium with a touch of caramel, Mexican with cinnamon and cayenne, oat-y with oak milk, chocolate with fresh mint, and even a choice to spike with booze. You can't go wrong with the Old Fashioned Hot Chocolate, a decadent mix of medium hot chocolate, milk chocolate– and cocoa nib–whipped ganache, and fluffy marshmallows. Life is short: Eat dessert first. The rotating dessert menu plays homage to childhood classics with a little Mindy magic. Death by chocolate is not a bad way to go, especially with the Flourless Chocolate Cake with hot chocolate presented three ways: frozen, capped with whipped, and poured with hot. Balance it all out with the "Shrimp Louie" Wedge with lettuce, plump grilled shrimp, crumbled egg, crispy bacon, and sliced avocados. Don't leave without trying the Mac & Cheese, silky, satiny, and absolutely comforting.

5

MARGIE'S CANDIES

Part candy store and part sit-down ice cream parlor, **MARGIE'S CANDIES** is one of Chicago's legendary spots that shouldn't be missed. The Poulos family has owned it for over nine decades, and it continues to be a popular destination for homemade candies and good ol' ice cream sundaes. Margie's Candies was named after the current owner's mom, Margie Michaels, who passed away in 1995. Peter George Poulos is the third-generation owner of the shop.

Music legends and celebrities including Aretha Franklin, the Beatles, Elvis, Marilyn Monroe, Meryl Streep, the Rolling Stones, Walt Disney, and more have visited Margie's Candies for their delightful desserts. Even Al Capone is said to have been a frequent patron.

Peruse the glass display cases of fudge, hand-dipped cherries, truffles, and turtles, or have a seat at one of the booths for a heavenly sundae. The Turtle Sundae has two scoops of French vanilla ice cream topped with nuts, whipped cream, wafer cookie, and a cherry with a side combo of caramel and fudge sauce. The old-fashioned ice cream parlor charm will make you feel nostalgic. It doesn't get more nostalgic than an Old-Fashioned Banana Split with French vanilla, chocolate, and strawberry ice cream garnished with pineapples, strawberries, nuts, whipped cream, wafer cookie, a cherry, and fudge sauce. All of the candies and ice cream are homemade, including the toppings. Make sure to bring your stretchy pants, because these sweet treats are decadent and indulgent. The World's Largest Sundae has a half gallon of ice cream—your choice (mix and match)—with all the trimmings. But wait, there's more!

If you're up for the challenge, try The Royal George with a whopping 25 scoops of ice cream. Take a friend . . . or 10 to try this monstrous bowl of goodness.

LE BOUCHON

The late chef Jean-Claude Poilevey and his wife Susanne opened **LE BOUCHON**, a charming French bistro, in 1993 in the Bucktown neighborhood. The word *authentic* is so overused in the restaurant industry that it's hard to be convinced if a place actually is. But when it comes to Le Bouchon, the word *authentic* could not be more fitting. From the owners to the food to the service, it's pure, reliable, and credible. Sadly, chef Jean-Claude Poilevey, who also owned La Sardine, passed away in a tragic auto accident in 2016, but his legacy of warmth, respect, and artistry lives on through his wife and three sons who oversee the restaurants today.

The food is traditional, and dishes are what you can expect to find in a *bouchon*. The meal starts with soft, pull-apart bread and butter. I always get the Soupe à l'Oignon Gratinée (onion soup), which is covered with a considerable amount of stretchable cheese. The Salade Lyonnaise is a classic with mixed greens, poached egg, lardons (lardy fat bacon), and mustard vinaigrette. I'm obsessed with the croutons and always eat them before digging into the salad. Don't judge! Bite into one and you'll understand what I am saying. The Truite Des Fjords en Croûte—ocean trout with English pea mousse wrapped in a delicate, flaky puff pastry with a light rosé beurre blanc—was simply incredible. Rotating specials are offered, like the Snail Boudin, snails enclosed into a cylindrical sausage decked with succulent shrimp, velvety polenta, and green garlic. I have seriously never had a bad meal here.

THE BRISTOL

THE BRISTOL is a Chicago essential for American fare and weekend brunch with impeccable service. As a leader in whole-animal butchery, they have been satisfying hungry carnivores everywhere since 2008 with their nose-to-tail approach. *Carbivores* and vegetarians, do not despair; the seasonal menu also highlights handmade pastas and glowing vegetables curated by executive chef and partner, Todd Stein (also of Formento's and Nonna's).

Love Cheetos? How about cheddar-dusted *chicharrones* paired with spicy mustard Steak Tartare? Chef said he was eating a bag of Cheetos one day, and it sparked the idea of incorporating cheddar dusted flavors with tartare instead of toast. Drop the mic. Stop monkeying around and get the Monkey Bread—buttery, savory dough puffs sit in a mini cast-iron pot. Pull apart and get in there with the dill butter. Order the plate-size Raviolo and dip the Monkey Bread in the brown butter—trust me. It's an insider tip I got specifically from the chef.

A gem of a drink is the Black Diamond cocktail with George Dickel Rye Whisky, Amaro Averna, lemon juice, grapefruit juice, and Angostura bitters. The Amish Half Chicken served on a bed of mustard dill spaetzle, covered in chicken jus, and layered with a crunchy salad is a staple and always in high demand. I am pretty sure people would riot if it were ever removed from the menu. Speaking of rioting, I would protest if they ever took the Basque Cake off the menu. Dramatic much? Yes, but the tart-pie-cookie-cake texture topped with seasonal fruit is so dreamy.

> On weekends we brunch and get the Mushroom Toast topped with a sunny-side up egg. End of story.

THE LINCOLN PARK CRAWL

1. Sit back and enjoy the show at **ALINEA**, 1723 N. HALSTED ST., CHICAGO, (312) 867-0110, ALINEARESTAURANT.COM

2. Enjoy the seasons at **BOKA**, 1729 N. HALSTED ST., CHICAGO, (312) 337-6070, BOKACHICAGO.COM

3. Satisfy your appetite at **GEMINI**, 2075 N. LINCOLN AVE., CHICAGO, (773) 525-2522, GEMINICHICAGO.COM

4. Sweeten your day at **SWEET MANDY B'S**, 1208 W. WEBSTER AVE., CHICAGO, (773) 244-1174, SWEETMANDYBS.COM

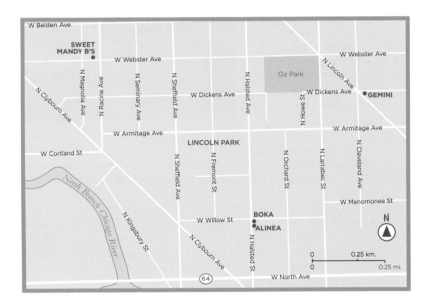

Lincoln Park

Food by the Park

LINCOLN PARK IS ONE OF THE BEST-KNOWN PARKS and neighborhoods in Chicago. The actual "park" is 1,200 acres and spans nearly 7 miles along the shores of Lake Michigan—from Ohio Street Beach up to Kathy Osterman Beach, where Lake Shore Drive ends. The city purposely made this valuable lakefront property a public park so it can be enjoyed and used by all. Where the Lincoln Park neighborhood and park meet are many public amenities, including Lincoln Park Zoo, Lincoln Park Conservatory, Theater on the Lake, the Chicago History Museum, the Peggy Notebaert Nature Museum, the Alfred Caldwell Lily Pool, the North Pond Nature Sanctuary, and North Avenue Beach.

The Lincoln Park neighborhood is north of Downtown. The city cemetery until the 1860s, Lincoln Park is today one of Chicago's most popular and vibrant neighborhoods, known for its numerous bars and restaurants. Home to DePaul University, Lincoln Park also has areas known to be some of Chicago's wealthiest. The diversity in residents is, of course, reflected by the wide range of restaurant options, from cheap eats to Chicago's perennial Michelin three-star winner, Alinea.

1

ALINEA

ALINEA, a Michelin three-star restaurant, is the most coveted restaurant in Chicago by legendary chef Grant Achatz His thought-provoking and thrilling approach to cooking has put Chicago on the worldwide dining map. I have been lucky enough to travel near and far to dine at the best restaurants in the world, but there is no experience that can compare to Alinea. With theatrics and science, Achatz takes you on a culinary journey that will leave you on the edge of your seat. It is a place everyone should experience at least once in his or her lifetime.

Alinea features three experiences: The Gallery, The Salon, and The Kitchen Table. The Gallery is the main dining room with a 16- to 18-course experience, while The Salon, located upstairs, features 10 to 14 courses. My preference is The Kitchen Table, a private room enclosed with a floor-to-ceiling window peeping into the kitchen. No menu is assigned, so sit back and enjoy the show. Be aware of your surroundings though. Everything has purpose and meaning. The orange centerpiece turns into dry ice fog, releasing a citrus scent, while a tabletop campfire burns, evoking nostalgic memories of the outdoors. Plating is always visionary and originative, and leaves you wondering what's going to happen next. The grand finale Paint dessert deserves a standing ovation. Multiple chefs come and slam, crack, throw, dust, and sprinkle on the table canvas, all to the beat of foot-tapping, hand-clapping music. The end result is an artistic dessert with foam, cotton candy, sauces, and more. Dig in!

2 BOKA

Since opening in 2003, **BOKA** has been a revered dining destination and one of the most celebrated restaurants in Chicago. With over 15 years in business, it is safe to say this flagship restaurant of the Boka Restaurant Group is a proven concept that stands the test of time. The main dining room is dark and mysterious, while the interior of the courtyard is whimsical. It gives off an Alice in Wonderland meets Enchanted Forest vibe. Lively greenery adorns the walls with quirky animal paintings.

Since joining in 2014, executive chef–partner Lee Wolen has been winning the hearts and stomachs of patrons and critics everywhere. Cold, Hot, and Entrées categorize Wolen's seasonal American menu. Strawberries must have been in season when I went, as they were highlighted in several dishes. Roasted strawberries, freeze-dried raspberries, and smoked brioche came together effortlessly with the asparagus and lightly smoked foie gras; the playful textures and flavors are beautifully presented. Summery red and green strawberries make an appearance in the Live Scallop Crudo, leaving subtle sweet and tart notes. The Charcoal Grilled Beets gave a fall vibe with the smokiness of the beets, pumpkin butter, and pumpkin seeds. The Whole Roasted Dry Aged Duck with foie gras sausage, onion, and cherries is made for two. To share or not to share is the big question. An 8-course tasting menu is also available.

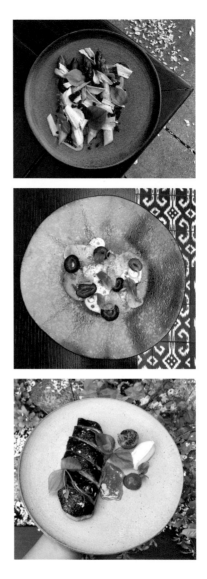

3

GEMINI

GEMINI is a quaint neighborhood restaurant satisfying the hungry appetites of many with a wide-ranging menu. Its foundation is rooted in Italian and French cuisines but using Midwestern ingredients and a made-from-scratch approach. The eclectic menu offers a little bit of everything, so it fits the taste of everyone. Set in a relaxed atmosphere with friendly service, it is a type of place you go for a no-frills night. During warmer months, the patio is an ideal spot to partake in adult drinking while the warmth of the sun touches your face. Grab their signature burger while you're at it; the pancetta crisp and Gemini aioli make this dish. Ah, life is good.

The presentation of the Chicken Tinga Nachos is similar to a passed appetizer at a fancy party, where the toppings are layered on the tortilla chip. It is not what you would expect of nachos, since it is carefully placed instead of piled high on the plate. One of the highlights on the menu is

the meaty Atlantic Swordfish Chop, which sits in a buttery lemon-serrano sauce and is served on the bone. The Steak Frites comes with your choice of top sirloin or filet, prepared with a port wine reduction sauce and beef bone marrow butter. The Key Lime "Magic Shell" sundae is spellbinding: A white chocolate shell drips over a big scoop of key lime ice cream surrounded by a peanut butter–and–graham cracker blondie and capped with toasted meringue and pineapples.

4

SWEET MANDY B'S

You can't help but smile when you walk into **SWEET MANDY B'S** with its pastel decor and "The best things in life are sweet" wall. This neighborhood bakery has been serving old-fashioned desserts since 2002. Cindy Levine's story starts in her home kitchen, where she made heavenly treats for her friends and family. The happiness it brought to them prompted her to open a small storefront, an inviting place where people could gather and experience that same joy. Named after her daughter, Amanda, and son, Brian, Sweet Mandy B's embodies childhood nostalgia in the sweetest way. Now under new ownership, Julie and Tommy Wang stay true to the classics while maintaining the welcoming atmosphere.

Sweet Mandy B's is most known for their cupcakes with soft-hued buttercream. The daily cake flavors are traditional—vanilla, chocolate, red velvet, carrot, and more—with a seasonal selection featuring pumpkin and gingerbread. Special-order cupcakes include riffs on familiar foods like french toast, peanut butter and jelly, turtle, and blueberry pancakes. The delicate-colored buttercream is also iced on top of buttery sugar cookies. Adorable cutout butter cookies are available for any occasion. For some stick-to-the-roof-of-your-mouth goodness, try the Peanut Butter Rice Krispies, with a thick sheet of milk chocolate. Other options include seasonal pies, personalized cakes, wedding cakes, and more. Whatever you choose, life is sweet.

THE LOGAN SQUARE CRAWL

1. *Buon appetito* at **OSTERIA LANGHE**, 2824 W. ARMITAGE AVE., CHICAGO, (773) 661-1582, OSTERIALANGHE.COM

2. Delight in pie at **BANG BANG PIE & BISCUITS**, 2051 N. CALIFORNIA AVE., CHICAGO, (773) 276-8888, BANGBANGPIE.COM

3. Take a slurp at **RAMEN WASABI**, 2101 N. MILWAUKEE AVE., CHICAGO, (773) 227-8180, WASABICHICAGO.COM

4. Brunch it up at **LULA CAFE**, 2537 N. KEDZIE BLVD., CHICAGO, (773) 489-9554, LULACAFE.COM

5. Heat it up at **MI TOCAYA ANTOJERIA**, 2800 W. LOGAN BLVD., CHICAGO, (872) 315-3947

6. Eat, Drink, Sleep at **LONGMAN & EAGLE**, 2657 N. KEDZIE AVE., CHICAGO, (773) 276-7110, LONGMANANDEAGLE.COM

7. Carb-load it up at **CELLAR DOOR PROVISIONS**, 3025 W. DIVERSEY AVE., CHICAGO, (773) 697-8337, CELLARDOORPROVISIONS.COM

8. Experience Macau at **FAT RICE**, 2957 W. DIVERSEY AVE., CHICAGO, (773) 661-9170, EATFATRICE.COM

9. Eat all the pastries at **THE BAKERY AT FAT RICE**, 2951 W. DIVERSEY AVE., CHICAGO, (773) 661-9544, EATFATRICE.COM/MENUS/THE-BAKERY

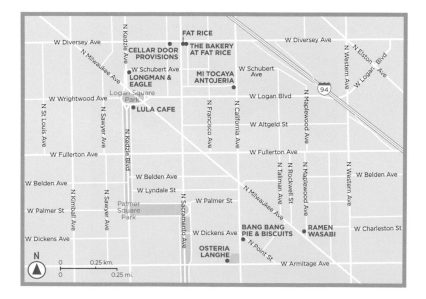

Logan Square

Livin' in a Hipsta's Paradise

LOGAN SQUARE, LOCATED ON THE NORTHWEST SIDE of Chicago, is considered one of the hippest neighborhoods in the city, and it's worth taking time to explore. It boasts vintage greystone homes, historic buildings, picturesque cityscapes, and beautiful boulevards, which are centered on the "square" (the three-way intersection of Milwaukee Avenue, Logan Boulevard, and Kedzie Boulevard). It is also the home of some of the best art galleries, music venues, restaurants, and bars in the city . . . without being pretentious.

The food and drink scene in Logan Square is eclectic and exhilarating. From exotic Macanese cuisine to charming Italian dining to tropical tiki bar cocktails, there is no shortage of variety. The restaurants and bars are casual, dishes approachable, and the chefs brilliant. The diverse culinary traditions meld with emerging food trends, unique dining experiences, and a chill vibe.

1 OSTERIA LANGHE

When it comes to Italian food, restaurants usually focus on northern or southern cuisine. The north features buttery sauces, meats, and cheeses, while the south highlights olive oil, pastas, and seafood. What is unique about **OSTERIA LANGHE** is that it is 100 percent dedicated to the region of Piemonte (or Piedmont), the only one of its kind in Chicago. Piemonte, meaning "at the foot of the mountain," is located in the northwestern part of Italy and known for its fine vineyards. Owner Aldo Zaninotto, a seasoned industry veteran, couples his restaurant experience and deep knowledge of wine to bring a truly special kind of Italian cuisine to Logan Square. To him, finding the right neighborhood was paramount, one where people and businesses support each other, similar to Piemonte, which played a key role in unifying the regions when Italy became a country. And that is your history lesson for today.

Foremost, enjoy a spritz in true Italian style. I drank my share of these citrusy, slightly bitter, bubbly drinks when I visited Italy. It is a great way to stimulate the appetite prior to your meal.

Chef Cameron Grant, a Scottish native, has been in the restaurant industry for two decades, including at the Michelin-starred La Ciau del Tornavento in Piemonte, Italy, where he learned how to make the very popular first-course dish Plin at Osteria Lange. Plin translates to "pinch," and the pillowy, hand-pinched ravioli are filled with pockets of La Tur and Parmesan cheeses and swim in a creamy butter-thyme sauce. If you want more—and I guarantee you will—you can purchase frozen Plin to take and make at home. The Peperoni Tonnato (not to be mistaken for pepperoni you put on your pizza) is a peppery twist on the classic *vitello tonnato*. In the version served here, roasted peppers (*peperoni*) are used instead of poached veal and dressed with tuna-citrus-caper aioli, arugula, and balsamic vinegar. There are two preparations of Piemontese beef—raw or poached—in Carne in Due Mondi. The flavors of the premium beef are spotlighted and enjoyed with a little grilled egg and crispy egg. Prosciutto-wrapped *coniglio* (rabbit) loin sits atop a bed of creamy polenta and is surrounded by truffle jus. You have a few dessert options to choose from, including the panna cotta with a sweet condensed milk caramel. *Delizioso!*

TRIFECTA TUESDAY

Get a three-course meal for $38 on Tuesday. Choose an appetizer, main, and dessert. Price does not include tax or gratuity.

BANG BANG PIE & BISCUITS

Every so often—let me rephrase that—more often than not, I crave pie. And when I do, I head out to **BANG BANG PIE & BIS-CUITS.** The minute you walk through the door, you get a whiff of the freshly baked pies and buttery biscuits that you wish you could capture in a scratch 'n' sniff sticker. Wait . . . was that weird? #sorrynotsorry

Owner Michael Ciapciak is no stranger to the restaurant world. He's worked in the industry for several prestigous names, including Gramercy Tavern and Blue Hill in New York. He was also a luxury food and hospitality critic and consultant for Forbes Travel Guides. Can I say dream job? After spending his career in fine dining, he decided to come back to his roots in the Midwest and serve approachable comfort food in a relaxed environment.

Their pies are incredible, and the rotating menu features both sweet and savory varieties. I usually go for something with chocolate or berries, but if you like key lime pie, their version is out of this world. The key lime custard is creamy, tangy, and all-around delightful.

For a savory option, the chicken potpie comes with generous portions of roasted chicken smothered in chicken gravy, carrots, peas, and celery in a flaky double crust. It is served in a cute little cast-iron skillet for your very own individual consumption, because you won't want to share. Your warm, buttery biscuits just got better with ham. The combination of the sweet maple-glazed smoked ham and biscuits with Dijon-chive butter is "intended to be a Midwestern riff on the simple Parisian treat of a baguette with ham and butter," Ciapciak says. The egg is an extra charge but worth every penny. Add a side of candied bacon, because bacon makes everything better. The thick-cut bacon with hints of smoky, spicy, and sweet will hook you immediately. How fancy are you feeling? Choose between the Not-So-Fancy straightforward bowl of cheddar grits; the Fancy bowl of cheddar grits with collard greens, poached egg, and hot sauce; or the Extra Fancy bowl of cheddar grits with shrimp or seasonal ingredients. I say always go for the Extra Fancy, because why not?

Can't decide between the pies? Get the Franken-pie, which is a whole pie constructed with a slice of each of the daily sweet pies.

RAMEN WASABI

RAMEN WASABI specializes in Japanese comfort food and ramen in a contemporary but laid-back environment. Owners Satoko Takeyama and Jee Kim opened in 2010 because they couldn't find any good ramen shops in Chicago. They wanted a place where you can get authentic Japanese ramen using premium ingredients.

Chicago winters can be unbearably brutal, with freezing temperatures and high wind speeds. I can't think of a better way to beat the cold weather blues than with a piping-hot bowl of ramen. The heritage Berkshire pork broth is carefully crafted for 45 hours, creating the ultimate bowl of Tonkatsu Ramen. The rich and milky broth pairs well with the tender noodles, topped with Berkshire pork belly, soft-boiled egg, marinated bamboo shoots, scallions, sesame seed, black wood ear mushrooms, and garlic oil, creating an impressive flavor profile. If you want a little extra kick, add the umami flavor bomb for $2 to boost the spice in your bowl. The Spicy Roasted Garlic Miso is also popular with all the accompaniments, including garlic chips and chile threads. For the blistering summer days, Ramen Wasabi offers Tsukemen, also known as dipping ramen; dip the cold noodles into the warm, deep-flavored broth, which is served in a separate bowl. These noodles are chewier and the broth thicker than regular ramen. Now excuse me while I go slurp a bowl of ramen.

While the ramen is the star of the menu, don't forget to try the Tokyo-style street food. Some crowd favorites are the Pork Belly Buns with braised Berkshire pork belly, organic romaine, sesame mayo, and scallions between a pillowy bun, as well as the Pork Belly and Kimchi Spring Rolls stuffed with Berkshire pork belly, kimchi, and glass noodles, and served with a house tartar sauce. The Sashimi Carpaccio is my go-to appetizer, with house ponzu, micro wasabi, roe, and truffle oil.

Check out the seasonal specials, including the Uni and Toro with grand fatty tuna tartare, chive, quail yolk, seaweed confetti, and real wasabi capped over rice. Mix all the ingredients together, wrap a piece of seaweed over the mixture, and enjoy!

4 LULA CAFE

LULA CAFE is your quintessential neighborhood spot for market-fresh artisan fare. Opened in 1999 by chef Jason Hammel, it was a pioneer in the dining scene in Logan Square as well as a leader in the farm-to-table dining movement before its popularization. What once was a small storefront with a home stove has now expanded into three storefronts. They continue to pack in the crowds with their visionary seasonally driven menu and carefree vibe. Open from 9 a.m. to late night (closed on Tuesday), it is a convenient place for any occasion. Lively bar available, so grab a cocktail, beer, or wine.

The menu is always evolving based on the ingredients, but it's consistently good. Whether studded with cranberries, speckled with poppy seeds, or swirled with chocolate, the house pastries are scrumptious treats. Wake up to a classic breakfast burrito: Thick chunks of potato, organic scrambled eggs, avocado, tomato, cheddar, salsa verde, and sour cream are wrapped in a warm flour tortilla. French toast is always a good idea, and the coconut brioche version is *n-utterly* splendid, with an appealing banana pastry cream and kaffir lime leaves in the caramel sauce. Lunch it up with friends over a '99 Turkey Sandwich, a notorious BLT with turkey, avocado, and chile aioli. Turn up the beets with the Beet Bruschetta with schmears of whipped goat cheese, marinated kale, shaved red onions, and smoked pecans.

> Lula Cafe is vegetarian-friendly and offers items like the Tofu and Vegetable Scramble with ginger-miso sauce and black sesame seeds.

MI TOCAYA ANTOJERIA

Chef-owner Diana Dávila returns to her Mexican roots and composes well thought-out dishes at **MI TOCAYA ANTOJERIA**. Mi Tocaya, meaning "my namesake" in Spanish, is a term of endearment when someone has the same name as oneself. This modest (seats 38) restaurant serves *antojeria*, "little cravings." Mi Tocaya is a unique reinvention of Mexican food with the immersion of new, old, and even the unfamiliar.

The seasonal menu features shareable plates, a couple of desserts, and handcrafted libations. Ask your server for a rundown of the menu since most of it is in Spanish. A light way to start your meal is with the Ensalada de Nopales, a splendidly composed plate of raw cactus, burrata, and *chicharrnes*. Heat things up with the Salpicón de Pollo, a Mexican-style pasta with a mix of diced chicken, hard-boiled egg, sugar snap peas, and a fiery salsa macha. Oh, and it's speckled with fried grasshoppers, an important part of the Mexican culinary heritage. Just keep an open mind! Insects are known to be nutritious, and their natural salty, acidic flavor is quite delicious. The Lobster Esquites with corn, crema enchilada, and epazote (an aromatic herb) are *a-maize-ing*! Go green and order the Fish con Mole Verde with romanesco broccoli, asparagus, and green mole. A full bar is available with draft and seasonal cocktails, beers, wine, and more.

There's a special Sunday dinner menu, which includes a toned-down version of the regular menu, as well as a few family favorites including the Habichuelas de la Olla con Carnitas with flavorful duck carnitas and green-tomato pico de gallo overlaying a bed of white beans.

6 LONGMAN & EAGLE

LONGMAN & EAGLE is a blast from the past and emulates the feel of an old town inn. The first floor features the rustic main dining area, where you can eat and drink to your hearts content. Tucked away in the rear of the building is a small bar known as OSB (off-site bar) where you can drink some more. They have a notable drink program with seasonal craft cocktails, an extensive whiskey selection, rare spirits, and small-batch wines. Grab a cold Negroni di Aquila with prosecco or a bubbly Hi Ball with bourbon or a solid Old Fashioned. If you get a little tipsy, stumble up to the second floor and rent one of the six charismatic rooms.

Executive chef Maxwell Robbins joined the team in 2018 but says he was a long-time, regular patron. Robbins brings new creative direction while still maintaining the core of Longman & Eagle's Midwestern traditions. The crowd-pleasing dishes still remain, like the Wild Boar Sloppy Joe and L&E Burger unsparingly stacked with pickles, onions, and cheese. He takes an uncomplicated approach to highlight key ingredients. The Falafel Scotch Egg lies atop tahini and chopped cucumbers—ingenious. How about some duck breast waddling in a puddle of soup jus with floating matzo balls and carrots? The Crispy Octopus is simply plated on a white dish to allow the playful presentation to really pop. You dip, I dip, we dip into the Smoked Trout Brandade with brie. All this dipping is making me tired; I will be upstairs catching some z's.

7 CELLAR DOOR PROVISIONS

Tucked away in a little corner of Diversey Avenue and Whipple Street is an unassuming farm-to-table restaurant that has the freshest breads, flakiest croissants, and the friendliest staff. It was love at first bite for me. *Here, please, just take my money.*

There is a strong sense of community here with an emphasis on supporting local businesses and farm communities. Everything **CELLAR DOOR PROVISIONS** serves is locally sourced and made in-house from scratch, including the spice blends, yogurts, and cheeses. Oh, and their breads are phenomenal. They are leavened with their sourdough starter and naturally fermented in small batches, creating a perfectly crackly crust and soft, tangy center. Slather on the house-made butter for a superb bite.

The rotating breakfast and lunch menu is handwritten on a mirror in a corner of the restaurant and regularly changes based on what is available from the farmers or what the staff feels like cooking. The food represents genuine expressions and thoughtful renditions of familiar dishes we love to eat.

The Pickled Fish, when paired with bread, brings to mind the taste of lox and bagels with the slight smokiness of the fish and velvety texture of the crème fraîche. The dish is elevated with the bright flavors of the cilantro oil and fresh vegetables. The restaurant strives to meet dietary needs, so there is always a vegetarian option like the Mushroom Tartine smeared with garlic confit and packed with enoki and pickled wood ear mushrooms. If you have never had a *cannele* from Cellar Door Provisions before, I recommend you run, don't walk, there. The creamy and custardy center is nestled in by the crunchy exterior and caramelized with beeswax and clarified butter. My biggest weaknesses are their croissants, especially the chocolate croissants . . . buttery and flaky with just the right amount of divine chocolate.

8 FAT RICE

Chef-owner Abraham Conlon opened **FAT RICE,** a Macanese restaurant, in 2012 with Adrienne Lo, sparked by their travels and their cultural backgrounds (Conlon, Portuguese, and Lo, Chinese). Their exceptionally creative Macanese menu draws upon a unique marriage of flavors from China and Portugal as well as ingredients and techniques from Africa, India, and Southeast Asia. They have received numerous accolades including the James Beard Best Chef: Great Lake 2018 award for chef Abraham Conlon.

There's a hidden cocktail lounge called The Ladies Room that sits behind a curtain in the back hallway of Fat Rice. They serve unique cocktails, rare wines, and sipping spirits in an exotic and loungy atmosphere.

The signature dish you must order is the Arroz Gordo, which literally means "fat rice." It is the celebratory dish of Macau, similar to paella. Their version is a melting pot of different regions and ingredients that creates a bountiful bowl that will stimulate your culinary senses. The hot clay pot is filled with overflowing layers of crispy sofrito-scented jasmine rice with sweet and sour raisins, chorizo, salted duck, curried thighs, char siu pork, linguiça sausage, prawns, steamed clams, tea eggs, chicken-fat-fried croutons, oil-cured olives, and pickled chiles. It is served with a side of mushroom soy and Diabo (devil) ghost pepper hot sauce.

While they are preparing the rice, order a few starters. The Pork and Ginger Dumplings are the essence of comfort food. Another great starter is the Bacalhau Da Vovó, a house-made salt cod spread lined with olives and pepper and served with *papo secos* (Portuguese rolls). Sharing is encouraged here with communal tables and an intimate setting.

THE BAKERY AT FAT RICE

Swing by **THE BAKERY AT FAT RICE** for some Asian-influenced treats, including sweet and savory breads, delicious pastries, and hand-pulled milk teas and coffee. Located next door to Fat Rice, it is an extension of owners Abraham Conlon and Adrienne Lo's successful Macanese restaurant but with a counter-service, grab 'n' go vibe. The decor is whimsical with brightly colored chairs, tropical flower accents, and birdcage-enclosed lights.

The globally inspired menu features ingredients from all over Asia, including the Philippines with the Ube Milk Bar (purple yam, shortbread, condensed milk jam, and coconut streusel) and Japan with the Miso Fudge Brownie (dark chocolate miso ganache and sweet salty candied almonds). Pastry chef Elaine Townsend has the extraordinary skill for mixing Eastern and Western ingredients to develop inventive combinations. The Ceylon Snickerdoodle is a blend of a Chinese egg yolk bun with a snickerdoodle cookie laced with Ceylon black tea sugar. It looks like a regular cookie from the outside, but when you break into it, you'll find a salted custardy egg yolk filling. Try their version of the Chicago-style hot dog, which has all the essential fixings, including a Vienna dog, tomatoes, relish, onions, and hot sport peppers, but it's baked on a Portuguese sweet dough and topped with Chinese hot mustard. The Pastel de Natas (Egg Tarts) are to die for!—a crumbly crust filled deep with a creamy, eggy center.

Bonus Crawl!

Logan Square Bar Crawl

From beer tastings to tiki lounge, there is always someplace to get your drink on in Logan Square. Check out my top spots.

1. **LOST LAKE**, 3154 W. DIVERSEY AVE., CHICAGO, (773) 293-6048, LOSTLAKETIKI.COM

2. **SCOFFLAW**, 3201 W. ARMITAGE AVE., CHICAGO, (773) 252-9700, SCOFFLAWCHICAGO.COM

3. **NAVIGATOR TAPROOM**, 2211 N. MILWAUKEE AVE., STE. 100, CHICAGO, (773) 687-9135, NAVIGATORTAPROOM.COM

4. **DEADBOLT**, 2412 N. MILWAUKEE AVE., CHICAGO, (773) 698-6101, DEADBOLTBAR.COM

5. **ESTEREO**, 2450 N. MILWAUKEE AVE., CHICAGO, (773) 360-8363, ESTEREOCHICAGO.COM

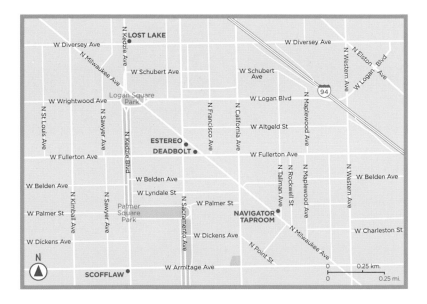

1 LOST LAKE

Need a beach vacation? Grab a tropical drink at **LOST LAKE** and get whisked away to a tiki paradise right here in Chicago. Inspired by 1930s Old Hollywood and the original Don the Beachcomber cafe, this cocktail bar is adorned with banana-leaf-printed wallpapers and thatched bamboo grass, giving it an island hut vibe.

Paul McGee, partner at Lost Lake, is the mastermind behind the creative cocktails. The drink menu includes original recipes of rum-infused concoctions, spiked punch, large-format cocktails (to share or not!), and daily selections including frozen daiquiris. The names of the drinks are as fun as the bar's looks, and you can come up with an amusing story: "Sail A Sea of Happiness" to "Your Special Island" at "Lost Lake" and hang out with a "Feejee Mermaid." Drink a "Prawn's Own Grog" or a "Bunny's Banana Daiquiri" and get "Hazy Lazy, Like, Kinda Crazy." The drinks have a kick, so make sure to soak it up with some Asian-inspired eats like the grilled chicken wings or pork dumplings.

SHHHH!

They offer a *"whisper menu"* with over 100 cocktails and special food items not on the regular menu. Available by request only.

2 SCOFFLAW

Located on Armitage Avenue, **SCOFFLAW** is a revered gin-focused cocktail bar by the Scofflaw Group (Danny Shapiro, Kristofer Nagy, and Andy Gould). The Victorian-style decor and built-in fireplace create a warm atmosphere while maintaining a familiar, neighborhood-like vibe. Shapiro heads the bar program, combining his wealth of knowledge and an astounding passion for his artistry. He is always pushing the boundaries to find new and exciting recipes to provide a constantly evolving, elevated experience. The cocktail menu is crafted around gin and rotates every three months. From fruity tones to decadent chocolate flavors, you will *gin-gle* all the way.

On top of the imaginative libations, they have a fabulous dining menu that goes beyond bar food. Executive chef Gabriel Freeman takes conventional flavors we recognize, like those in a BLT, and transforms them into BLT butter or adds crunch to deviled eggs with chicken cracklings. Even salads and tartines have whimsical twists. Who thinks of throwing onion ash and flax crackers on toast? Freeman does, and it's brilliant.

3 NAVIGATOR TAPROOM

Don't worry, *beer* happy at **NAVIGATOR TAPROOM,** a self-serve beer and wine taproom that opened in 2017. Owners Tim Enarson and Erik Swanson merge the concept of a Napa Valley tasting room with a brewery for a fun atmosphere where you can roam around and try different craft brews and wines. Start with a Navigator card with an RFID chip that allows you to tap on the screen and pour as you desire. It is kind of like an ATM machine, but instead of money, you get alcohol. Hip, *hops*, hooray!

They feature 36 beers, 8 wines, and 4 ciders arranged from light to dark with tasting notes. Their selection is vast, with American lagers, German pilsners, Belgium ales, and more. The software tracks your consumption and you pay by the ounce at the end. Feel free to try as many as you want or to stick to your favorites. Please note that by law they do have to check in after you reach 32 ounces, so make sure to limit your *pour* decisions. They have a small food menu from Serai, a neighboring Malaysian restaurant, but you can bring in your own food as well. Complimentary popcorn and pretzels are available for snacking.

TIP

Get the gang together and head out for their Beer & Board Games on Thursday starting at 6:30 p.m.

4 DEADBOLT

Dance to the beats of hip-hop, get down to the rhythms of funk, feel the groove of soul, and bust out the Carlton to R&B. Just kidding. Omit that last part. My point . . . music is life at **DEADBOLT** with rotating resident DJs. And, when coupled with energizing cocktails, you know you're in for a good time.

Partners Anshul Mangal, Shin Thompson, and Dustin Drankiewicz took over the former Two Way Lounge, a dive bar that operated in the neighborhood for over 50 years. Mangal and Thompson own the popular ramen shop Furious Spoon next door, so it was an opportune location. They rehabbed most of the space but tried to salvage as much as possible from the original. What once was the bandstand is now the stage for live DJs. The dim lights, leather booths, and dark wood heighten the cozy, moody vibe. Drankiewicz champions the beverage program and curates cocktails focused on the classics but with a fresh feel. The drinks rotate regularly, but you can expect creations like the mezcal with herbs, cosmo infused with aromatics, and pisco with berries or pumpkin, depending on the season. You can even get a couple of cocktails on draft that can be ordered in a single-serve or pitcher option. The Horse's Neck is a #1 seller in which they take the staff's favorite cocktail, carbonate it, and then serve in a bottle. Now, if only they had a wind machine so you can practice your Beyoncé moves. I will make sure to put that in the suggestion box.

5

ESTEREO

Feel the island vibes at **ESTEREO**, an all-day bar on the corner of Milwaukee and Sacramento Avenues. Enjoy coffee and cocktails or vice versa any time of day starting at 12 p.m. until late night. The atmosphere is eclectic with Latin calypso sounds and Caribbean aura. During warmer months, they keep it breezy and open the garage doors, which are attached to three of their walls. The elongated, triangular-shaped bar sits in the center of the room with plenty of seating wrapping around it. Isolated to the side are some small, round high-top tables if you want a little privacy.

The drinks are designed to highlight the main spirit and are categorized in that fashion. You can order from Pisco, Mezcal, Rum, Tequila, Cachaça, and more options, which are showcased in colorful letters on a whiteboard wall. The rum cocktail when I went had aguardiente and fig cranberry, and the Cachaça drink had passion fruit and grapefruit juices with cinnamon. Ingredients are out of the ordinary, like blood orange plus walnut, coconut-date horchata, and papaya (*fruta bomba*) bitters. If you're just not sure what to get, try the Breezy, which comes in a white plastic cup. Pick your spirit, then yerba maté, house Falernum, lime, and bubbles are mixed in. The icy, frosty Frozen slushies are great for chillin' in the summer. Vacation mode is in full effect here.

THE AVONDALE CRAWL

1. Hang out at **SON OF A BUTCHER BY WHISK**, 2934 W. DIVERSEY AVE., CHICAGO, (773) 687-9709, SOBUTCHER.COM

2. Stack 'em high at **KUMA'S CORNER**, 2900 W. BELMONT ST., CHICAGO, (773) 604-8769, KUMASCORNER.COM

3. Take a lunch break at **CAFE TOLA**, 3324 N. CALIFORNIA AVE., CHICAGO, (773) 293-6346, CAFETOLA.COM

4. Cluck on over to **HONEY BUTTER FRIED CHICKEN**, 3361 N. ELSTON AVE., CHICAGO, (773) 478-4000, HONEYBUTTER.COM

5. Soar high at **PARACHUTE**, 3500 N. ELSTON AVE., CHICAGO, (773) 654-1460, PARACHUTERESTAURANT.COM

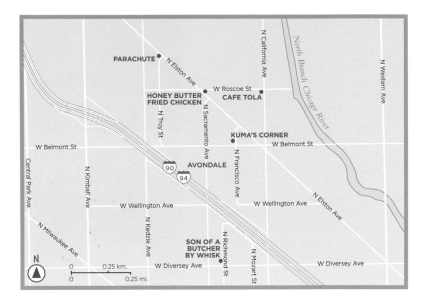

Avondale

Cultural Melting Pot

AVONDALE, ALSO KNOWN AS CHICAGO'S "POLISH VILLAGE," is a large neighborhood located on the northwest side of the city. This working-class community was once home to several manufacturing companies, like Bally Manufacturing, Dad's Root Beer, Florsheim Shoes, and Yardley Created Plastics, which helped Avondale earn its place as the "neighborhood that built Chicago." Today you will still find a number of Polish sausage shops, bakeries, and restaurants, but Avondale is also home to many Latino, Filipino, and former Soviet bloc communities.

The burgeoning restaurant scene helped Avondale gain recognition in 2017 from Lonely Planet as one of the "Hot 'hoods in the US: 10 neighborhoods you need to visit." The area doesn't boast fancy hotels or tourist attractions, but it offers a gritty, cool vibe that has not yet been overcome by the hipster nature of neighboring Roscoe Village and Logan Square. A sundry of restaurants have opened, ranging from burger and fried chicken joints to a Michelin-star award winner. Avondale is worth the visit, and I am certain more deliciousness will continue to pop up in this 'hood.

1

SON OF A BUTCHER BY WHISK

SON OF A BUTCHER BY WHISK is a welcoming, neighborhood spot for a chill night out for cold drinks and satisfying bar food. Chefs-owners Rick and David Rodriguez took over what was formerly known as Son of a Butcher. They kept the name to pay tribute to the previous owner's grandfather, who was a butcher, revamped the menu, and reawakened it as Son of a Butcher by Whisk, after their popular brunch/breakfast spot called Whisk (two locations). The Rodriguez brothers started in the food industry as dishwashers, worked their way up to line cooks, and now they're living the dream with three restaurants to their names. They were limited to what they could serve at Whisk, and this space was exactly what they were looking for in their expansion. It is a dinner-only joint with brunch on the weekends and a menu highlighting smoked meats, burgers, and Mexican flavors . . . comfort food at its finest.

Chef Rick Rodriguez says the menu is focused on what they like to eat, things they would serve if you came over to their house, while catering to the large Spanish community in the neighborhood. The Salsa + Pico + Queso is an excellent starter and perfect for sharing. The fresh, house-made salsas and pico de gallo are dippin' delightful, while the *chicharrones* add a fun, crunchy twist. The nachos come loaded with your choice of protein (barbecue brisket, carnitas, chicken, or steak), cheese sauce, fresh jalapeños, and pico de gallo. Every day is Fry-day with the Masa Steak Fries, house-made Maseca fries, skirt steak, avo-

cado salsa, sour cream, and Cotija cheese. Get piggy with it and order the Piggy Pops, cubes of fried pork belly on a stick with avocado salsa, pickled red onion, and Cotija cheese. My team member Lisette, who is Mexican, said the Street Corn is legit, pure joy on a stick with mayo, queso Cotija, and Tajín *clasico* seasoning.

KUMA'S CORNER

Rock out, pig out, and roll out. At **KUMA'S CORNER**, metal music and burgers go hand in hand. There is loud music blasting in the background and gory movies playing on the screen, but people swarm to the flagship location in Avondale for their monstrous burgers named after metal bands and craft beers. I wouldn't recommend going if you are looking for a romantic date spot or a place to take your kids, but it is definitely somewhere you will want to check out for a ridiculously tasty burger that's the size of your face.

The Famous Kuma is their signature burger, with applewood-smoked bacon, melty cheddar cheese, lettuce, tomato, red onion, and a farm-fresh fried egg, because you should always #putaneggonit. If you love breakfast food, try the Souvein, deep-fried blackened chicken tenders with applewood-smoked bacon, cheddar cheese, Belgian waffle strips, maple syrup drizzle, and raspberry aioli. OMFG. Get High on Fire with roasted red peppers, prosciutto, grilled pineapples, sweet chile paste, and sriracha hot sauce. Although "fire" is in the name, it's actually not that spicy. The grilled pineapples, roasted red peppers, and the chile paste give it sweetness with a tartness from the fruit. It has a mild spice but nothing that will get you high on fire.

They feature a different burger of the month, an off-the-wall creation with innovative ingredients, such as burgers topped with frizzled beets

or bacon wasabi coleslaw. How about a burger piled with a Mae Ploy chili pancake and teriyaki Spam? I tried the Bell Witch burger, an Impossible vegan burger that can be made with a beef patty, pecan-wood-smoked pork shoulder bacon, and regular cheese for all you carnivores. Quite honestly, try it the vegan way; you won't even miss the meat. The consistency of the vegan patty mimics the beef patty, and it's spread with a hearty sundried tomato ketchup and layered with vegan Colby Jack cheese, whiskeysoaked dill pickles, lettuce, tomato, and fresh dill.

Save room for the savory, create-your-own mac and cheese sprinkled with bread crumbs and scallions. You can have two add-ins, including prosciutto, corn, chili, andouille sausage, bacon, broccoli, caramelized onions, chicken, and more. *Warning:* Falling into a food coma after eating here is highly likely. Now that you are nice and full, give to a good cause. Kuma's big on supporting local causes and donates to different charities every month. Ask your server about it.

CAFE TOLA

There are some big shoes to fill when you open in the former iconic Hot Doug's space, where people waited in long lines to try one of Doug Sohn's gourmet dogs (I waited 8 hours the week they closed). Frank Meats Patty took the space for a short time and closed abruptly after less than a year. Currently, **CAFE TOLA** occupies the space, and it is working out well for them. Cafe Tola's original location is on Southport in Lakeview, where their award-winning empanadas popularized them. Mentored by her grandparents, co-owner Victoria Salamanca started cooking at a young age. She spent her summers in Florida, where her grandparents lived. They were fruit and vegetable pickers, and her grandmother taught her to cook. Salamanca named the restaurant Tola because it is the name she shares with her grandmother. They would refer to her grandmother as Doña Tola, and she was called Tolita.

Salamanca and her co-owner/husband chose Avondale as their second location because they live in the neighborhood with their six kids. At this location, Salamanca cooks the food she wants to eat, while providing the workers in the neighborhood early hours with warm home-cooked meals in an informal atmosphere. Her grandfather always told her to give people good full meals and not expensive bites. Check out the cool art on the

wall while waiting for the food. The vibe has a retro feel with murals of Kanye West, Michael Jordan, and Walter Payton as well as a display of

vintage toys, including Transformers and Godzilla. Order at the counter and don't miss out on the empanadas: The fried half-moon-shaped treats are bulging with fillings like spinach and cheese, *rajas* (creamy poblano pepper strips) and cheese, and beans and cheese.

If you're reading this, buy me tacos. Two corn tortillas are covered with mounds of protein like *al pastor* (marinated pork), skirt steak, *birria* (barbecued goat), chicken verde, *pancita* (pork belly), and seasonal veggies with an assortment of toppings. They also have a fantastic chicken mole, served with a larger flour tortilla and covered in an abundance of a mild peanut- and cocoa-based mole. The Nopales (cactus) is mixed with pork and black beans and served with corn tortillas. Best way to describe nopales is that they

TIP

For online orders, try the Dealer's Choice: You'll save $2 on three empanadas if you let your barista choose the flavors for you.

taste like asparagus but with a slippery texture that's great for your digestive system. Notch up the spice with the Queso Flameado with roasted poblano peppers, assorted mushrooms, onion, and Chihuahua cheese, and spiked with a little tequila. You might cry from the heat, but they're happy tears.

4 HONEY BUTTER FRIED CHICKEN

The name alone should entice you to go. What's not to like about **HONEY BUTTER FRIED CHICKEN**? I'm hungry just thinking about it. The best part of HBFC—or one of the best parts—is that they stand behind the philosophy that you should know where your food comes from and you should feel good about what you're eating. This means they use only cage-free, humanely raised, antibiotic-free chickens from a reputable source, and they fry it in a non-GMO, trans-fat-free canola oil. My 15-month-old, who has been eating organic all her life, loves it, and I am completely fine letting her eat a few pieces because I know there aren't any chemicals or hormones in the food. The cornmeal in the muffins, cheese in the mac 'n' cheese, and honey for the butter—each ingredient is thoughtfully sourced from local farmers and businesses with the same values.

This is a counter-service spot with lots of seating and a spacious patio area. The fried chicken comes in pieces, strips, sandwiches, and add-ons for salads. First time here? Start off with the pieces, which come in quantities of 2, 4, or 8 and are served with the most divine corn muffins. Slather on the honey butter; it literally melts in your mouth. I want to scoop the whole thing and eat it like ice cream (#savage). Side options include mashed potatoes, grits, creamed corn, and my favorite—the dairy-free, gluten-free, and vegan Kale & Cabbage Slaw. HBFC is really good about accommodating any dietary restrictions or allergies. The Buffalo Mac 'n Cheese, with fried chicken, honey buffalo sauce, and fried crunchies, is enough to share

as a side. A sure thing is the chicken wings. Choose between Honey Buffalo or the monthly special. Either way you can't go wrong, because the real clucking goodness comes from the nonoily, super-crispy, lightly battered wings. The "OG" Fried Chicken Sandwich is a signature dish, with fried chicken strips, candied jalapeño mayo, and crunchy slaw busting out of a buttery soft bun.

CALLING ALL VEGETARIANS!

You can swap out the bird for local, non-GMO fried tofu strips on any sandwich.

5 PARACHUTE

PARACHUTE flies high with accolades from Michelin (one star) and soaring recognitions from *Bon Appétit* and the *Chicago Tribune*, among many more. Chefs-owners and husband-and-wife team Johnny Clark and Beverly Kim opened Parachute in 2014 as a last-ditch effort to fulfill their dream of operating a restaurant together. Although Avondale didn't have much going on at the time, they chose the neighborhood because it wasn't biased or stereotyped in any way. Plus, the rent was affordable, so they took a chance. You may recognize Kim, who's appeared on Bravo's *Top Chef*, where she was known for her Korean-inspired food. She still cooks with Korean ingredients and flavors, but Parachute's menu melds the two chefs' backgrounds together to create Korean-American fare with a modernistic perspective. You will find hints of familiar traditional flavors presented in an approachable way. The menu is seasonal, using products only at their peak, and changes nightly with a focus on highlighting the main ingredients.

Bada bing! The Baked Potato Bing Bread has been on the menu since Day One, and it is a must-order. It comes in half or full order, but go for the full . . . just sayin'. Get *bready* for the warm, soft bread loaded with hearty chunks of potatoes, bacon, and scallions. Slather on the sour-cream butter for pure ecstasy. The raw yellowfin tuna is bright and refreshing with citrus and acidic notes and a smooth crunch from the young almonds. Deep smoky flavors exude from

the Smoked Yuba, paperthin, spongy tofu skewered on a wooden stick and surrounded by an earthy broth of stewed French beans and mushrooms. Black bean sauce and fresh cucumbers cover the delicately battered soft-shell crabs; the flavors remind me of a lighter version of *jjajangmyeon,* a Korean-Chinese noodle dish with a black bean sauce. The hanger steak, cooked to just the right temperature, is perfectly juicy and tender and topped with meaty tomatoes and pickled anchovies. *Patbingsu,* a Korean shaved ice dessert, is a childhood favorite that I remember making with a Snoopy Sno-Cone Machine. Para-

chute's version is far more sophis-ticated, with condensed milk, raspberries, blackberries, mochi, and puffed rice, but it still evokes my nostalgia from eating it as a child. I know people don't usually think of wine with Korean food, but Parachute has a wonderful wine program with a focus on natural wines from smaller vineyards with notes that pair well with the spices of Korean food.

THE LAKEVIEW & WRIGLEYVILLE CRAWL

1. Explore coastal Spain at **MFK.**, 432 W. DIVERSEY PKWY., CHICAGO, (773) 857-2540, MFKRESTAURANT.COM

2. Holy crepes at **THE CREPE SHOP**, 2928 N. BROADWAY, CHICAGO, (773) 857-0018, THECREPESHOPCHICAGO.COM

3. Wing it at **CRISP**, 2940 N. BROADWAY, CHICAGO, (773) 697-7610, CRISPONLINE.COM

4. Globetrot the world at **MORTAR & PESTLE**, 3108 N. BROADWAY, CHICAGO, (773) 857-2087, MORTARANDPESTLECHICAGO.COM

5. Lounge around at **ELLA ELLI**, 1349 W. CORNELIA AVE., CHICAGO, (773) 935-3552, ELLAELLICHICAGO.COM

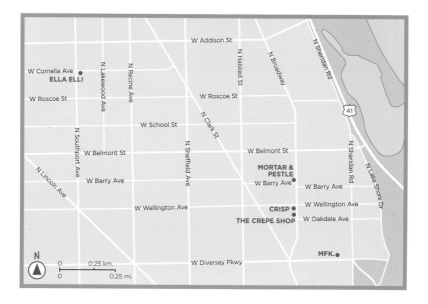

Lakeview & Wrigleyville

Keep It Casual

LAKEVIEW IS ONE OF CHICAGO'S MOST POPULAR NEIGHBOR-HOODS and has a little something for everybody. While some neighborhoods have only a couple commercial corridors, Lakeview boasts six for shopping, eating, drinking, and the arts—Belmont Avenue, Broadway Street, Clark Street, Halsted Street, Lincoln Avenue, and Southport Avenue—each with its own vibe.

The neighborhood is split into Lakeview East and Lakeview West, and the only corridor that runs through both is Belmont Avenue, which is a bit edgy with eclectic offerings: great places to eat and drink, army surplus stores, fashion boutiques, tattoo parlors, cigar shops, comedy and performance theaters, music venues, and more.

In Lakeview East, you have Broadway where there is a variety of restaurants and bars. Then you have Halsted Street (Northalsted), also known as Boystown, which has a thriving LGBT community and Wrigleyville—the area around Wrigley Field. Go, Cubs, go! Even before the 2016 World Series, Wrigleyville was undergoing considerable renovation. A decade ago, going to Wrigleyville bars was my worst nightmare, but now I love going; the amenities are so much nicer—the new hotel, public areas, and, of course, the restaurants.

In Lakeview West, the intersection of Lincoln, Southport, and Wellington Avenues is called Lincoln Hub, where the city is trying to expand parks and public spaces and make it more pedestrian-friendly to help local businesses. Southport is a bit of a "stroller alley" filled with family-friendly restaurants, bars, boutiques, major retail fashion chains, and Chicago's first Amazon Bookstore.

1

MFK.

Explore coastal Spain at **MFK.** for some seafood-centric eats. Located at basement level, the modest-size restaurant is a great getaway from the stresses of daily life. Owners Sari Zernich-Worsham and Scott Worsham (also of Bar Biscay) named the restaurant after the late M. F. K. Fisher, a well-known food writer with a career that spanned over 60 years. Fisher would often use food as a cultural metaphor, which was dismissed by others for many years.

There's a special type of culture and love of food at mfk. The atmosphere is designed for socializing and the food made for sharing. Grab a cocktail, like a Hawaiian Margarita (tequila, mescal, chorizo, pineapple, lemon), and browse through the menu. Broken out by One, Two, Three, and Dessert, the menu starts with smaller bites and proceeds to progressively larger dishes. You may not understand what all the ingredients mean, but keep an open mind and delve right in. The Suzuki Crudo is a delightful bite of squid ink, tostada, and guacamole. For the Mussels Escabèche, chèvre is lathered on top of thick, crusty bread and holds the piquillo pepper and mussels. The cauliflower dish is bursting with surprising flavors you normally wouldn't expect with this vegetable from the pickled sweet peppers and slight saltiness from the breadcrumbs. Refashioned from the classic, the Tortilla Española is made with salt cod brandade and topped with frisée.

2 THE CREPE SHOP

Brothers-owners Marius and Peter Toader always dreamed of opening a coffee shop and being immersed in a community. But instead of a traditional coffee shop, they wanted something distinctive, and **THE CREPE SHOP** was born. The brothers don't have any formal training as chefs, but both love to cook, and crepes were plausible to them. Paris-style street food combined with a sense of community makes for a charming spot in Lakeview for freshly made food and conversations over coffee.

The counter-service spot is small and narrow but comfy and snug with long communal tables. The various flavor combinations are posted on the wall on the right and include both savory and sweet crepes. Start your morning right with the ever-popular Lox crepe with smoked salmon, herb cream cheese, tomato, onions, capers, and lemon or a classic Ham & Cheese crepe with Black Forest ham, fontina cheese, and Mornay sauce, and topped with an egg. Caffeinate yourself with a house-made matcha or mocha latte. My all-time favorite is the Nutella crepe with strawberries. Nutella over Nutella anyone? Stuffed with cheesecake filling and topped with a three-berry coulis, the Wildberry Cheesecake is *berry* good. The owners are constantly experimenting with new flavors and are very receptive to suggestions, so if you have something specific in mind, let them know.

3

CRISP

A quick-service restaurant specializing in Korean-influenced comfort food, **CRISP** is home to some of the best fried chicken, known as KFC (Korean Fried Chicken), in the city. The hormone-free chickens are pressured cooked and double fried and tossed (if desired) in a secret house-made sauce: Choose between the Seoul Sassy, Crisp BBQ, or Buffalo. My favorite is the Seoul Sassy, a sweet sauce with ginger, soy, garlic, and other spices. It is owner Jae Lee's family recipe that has been handed down over many generations. The Crisp BBQ is a little spicy, sweet, and smoky, while the Buffalo is what you would expect from buffalo sauce. A Plain Jane version of chicken is available, too, which is seasoned but without sauce.

Also super popular here is the Buddha Bowl, their version of the Korean bibimbap (mixed rice). Pick your protein (chicken, beef, or none) and size. Baby Buddha is a bowl of rice topped with 4 types of veggies, a fried egg, and Buddha bowl sauce (gochujang). The Original Bad Boy Buddha has 8 veggies, while the Big Boy Buddha has 12. The portions are large especially the protein-packed bowls like the Seoul Steak Bowl as well their sizeable Seoul Sensation Korean burrito, which are excellent options if you are super hungry.

4 MORTAR & PESTLE

Chef-owner Stephen Ross is doing everything right at **MORTAR & PESTLE**, with an internationally inspired menu rooted in tradition. Ross never imagined that the building where he used to bring his chef's coat to be dry-cleaned would eventually be a restaurant he could call his own. The chef comes from a fine-dining background but takes a simpler approach of getting back to the basics. He is committed to making everything by hand, using only the finest ingredients. Focused on breakfast, brunch, and lunch, Ross takes you through Asia, Cuba, the Middle East, and beyond with no passport needed.

Let's head to France for some Foie Gras French Toast: Foie gras torchon sits comfortably in the center of the thick, pillowy brioche toast, dusted with bacon confectioners' sugar. Now you're talking my language. And, since eating more foie gras never hurt no one, the Foie Gras & Eggs, blanketed with shaved truffles, is a must. Journey to Asia for some Breakfast Fried Rice with bacon, ham, and egg in a soy-sesame sauce and served with kimchi. Adventure off to Switzerland for the Bircher Muesli, a nutritious bowl of walnuts, granola, berries, and brûléed banana. Head back to the States to Alaska: A lightly toasted English muffin is piled with juicy Alaskan king crab, crested with poached eggs, and covered in sriracha hollandaise.

> **I'M LOVIN' IT**
>
> A riff on the popular sandwich at the Golden Arches, the McNelson is pork sausage, egg, and cheese packed between maple-infused pancakes.

5 ELLA ELLI

ELLA ELLI, located in the heart of Lakeview, is a swanky, neighborhood spot by 4 Star Restaurant Group (Tuco and Blondie, Crosby's Kitchen, Remington's). The 2,200-square-foot, 75-seat restaurant has a charming 1920s vibe, with a lounge area perfect for cocktails. Try a Basil Limone, a citrusy vodka drink with limoncello, lemon, and basil, or an Old Fashioned with essential oils. The Hemingway is made with pamplemousse and grapefruit, while the Piquant has a kick from the chile-infused Aperol.

Chef Dan Harris says the Mediterranean-inspired food has Californian influences and is meant to pair with the cocktails. The Avocado Toast with poached egg is reminiscent of an everything bagel with the seasoning speckled on top. Vegetables and salads are real standouts like the Salt Roasted Carrots with za'atar, harissa, and pickled celery, or the Baby Gem Salad with green goddess yogurt and fried bread croutons. Wonderful bright colors pop off the plate of Peas Carbonara with black pepper, mascarpone, prosciutto, and cured egg yolk. The bold flavors from the blistered cherry tomatoes, garlic, and chiles balance out the light taste of the Mediterranean Sea Bass. The Italian word *scottadito* translates to "burn fingers," and you just may do that because you can't resist the Lamb Scottadito with herbed yogurt and harissa. And, because desserts are an

important part of this crawl, get your hands on the Profiteroles with French Vanilla Ice Cream and Espresso Chocolate.

Bonus Crawl!

Wrigleyville Bar Food Crawl

Chicago is a city that loves their sports team, no matter if they win or lose. Wrigley Field is located right in Wrigleyville, and you can expect swarms of people during game days. Here are few places to get your drink and eat on.

1. **RIZZO'S BAR & INN**, 3658 N. CLARK ST., CHICAGO, (773) 799-8161, RIZZOSBARANDINN.COM

2. **BUDWEISER BRICKHOUSE TAVERN**, 3647 N. CLARK ST., CHICAGO, (773) 377-4700, BRICKHOUSETAVERNCHI.COM

3. **MURPHY'S BLEACHERS**, 3655 N. SHEFFIELD AVE., CHICAGO, (773) 281-5356, MURPHYSBLEACHERS.COM

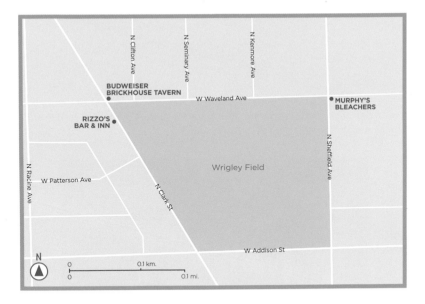

1

RIZZO'S BAR & INN

The Rizzo family has been an integral part of Chicago's history since 1946. It all started with Vincent Angel Rizzo, an Italian immigrant from Sicily. Cubs Park Service Station (CPSS) originally opened as a gas station with an interconnecting auto repair shop and car wash. As the neighborhood grew, the business evolved. Located near Wrigley Field, they began parking cars for game attendees and players, which soon became a popular local hangout. In 2017, Vincent's grandsons turned the parking lot into **RIZZO'S BAR & INN**.

Go big or go home at Rizzo's. The large-format offerings are supersized to the max. The giant pretzel is served with house-made whole-grain mustard, cheese sauce, and jelly preserves. A whole pound of mozzarella cheese is used to create giant logs of mozzarella sticks. Does that mean I'll gain a pound if I eat all of these? Hot diggity dog, there's a colossal corn dog, too. It gives new meaning to the phrase "jumbo dogs." The Trash Can Nachos are piled high with house-made cheese, fresh jalapeños, black beans, red onions, sour cream, pico de gallo, and guacamole. And, wait for it . . . The Notorious, a whopping 72-ounce burger with mayo, American cheese, pickles, red onion, tomato, lettuce, and bacon. I nearly threw out my back carrying it. Unless you are into competitive eating, I highly recommend you share.

Enjoy the over-the-top burger creations, which rotate during game weeks. The Burger X comes stacked with a 24-hour braised Wagyu short rib, bacon, and Grand Cru cheese between an ash bun.

2 BUDWEISER BRICKHOUSE TAVERN

Located in Gallagher Way, **BUDWEISER BRICKHOUSE TAVERN** is a lively pub-style restaurant by Four Corners Tavern Group and Hickory Street Capital. Named after the beloved Chicago Cubs broadcaster Jack Brickhouse (known for his signature "Hey, hey"), the tavern pays homage to his legacy with a fun and energetic vibe. The massive 15,000-square-foot multilevel space boasts 4 bars and multiple indoor and outdoor spaces overlooking Wrigley Field. Grab a summery drink and enjoy the view.

Budweiser Brickhouse Tavern offers an expansive food menu with riffs on Chicago favorites by Four Corners corporate chef Ryan Devitt. Nothing says Chicago favorite like a Chicago Polish Dog with all the fixings. The signature Buffalo Chicken Waffle Cone is a playful presentation of buffalo chicken bites in a fresh waffle cone sprinkled with crumbles of blue cheese. Get loaded on the Loaded Potato Bites, a unique twist on a classic baked potato. Specialty sandwiches are offered, including the Hot Fried Chicken and Brickhouse Bacon. Never say no to desserts, especially those made by the talented Four Corners's corporate pastry chef Amy Arnold. Her creations are photoworthy so take a pic first, then devour.

Gallagher Way owned by the Ricketts family is a great destination for year-round activities including festivals, farmers' markets, movie nights, and more. Located adjacent to Wrigley Field, it's also a hot spot for food, drinks, and game day activities.

3 MURPHY'S BLEACHERS

MURPHY'S BLEACHERS, formerly operated as Ernie's Bleachers (1930s) and Ray's Bleachers (1960s), is a historic bar that has been a go-to destination for Cubs fans and neighbors. Jim Murphy purchased the place in 1980, and through the years he has renovated it to feature a rooftop beer garden. Located right across the street from Wrigley Field's bleachers section, you'll be in the center of all the game-day action.

There's an extensive beer list featuring both draft and bottles from Midwestern brewers and beyond, with frequently changing seasonal and specialty beers. If beer is not your thing, they have hard ciders, whiskey, wine, and more. The food menu is uncomplicated and straightforward with Starters & Sides, Pizza, and Sandwiches. Nibble on some buffalo chicken wings served with crunchy celery sticks. Classic bar fare is offered, including a cheeseburger with bacon and a ¼-pound Angus beef hot dog served Chicago style. For something lighter, the chicken Caesar wrap is abundantly stuffed with chicken breast, romaine, Parmesan, fresh croutons, and housemade dressing. All sandwiches and wraps come with your choice of fries, tots, homemade potato salad, chips, or cottage cheese.

THE ANDERSONVILLE & EDGEWATER CRAWL

1. Hop on over to **HOPLEAF**, 5148 N. CLARK ST., CHICAGO, (773) 334-9851, HOPLEAF.COM

2. Indulge in treats at **GEORGE'S ICE CREAM & SWEETS**, 5306 N. CLARK ST., CHICAGO, (773) 271-7600, GEORGESICECREAMANDSWEETS.COM

3. Enjoy Southern cooking at **BIG JONES**, 5347 N. CLARK ST., CHICAGO, (773) 275-5725, BIGJONESCHICAGO.COM

4. Soul for Seoul **PASSEROTTO**, 5420 N. CLARK ST., CHICAGO, (708) 607-2102, PASSEROTTOCHICAGO.COM

5. Howl with joy at **LITTLE BAD WOLF**, 1541 W. BRYN MAWR AVE., CHICAGO, (773) 942-6399, LITTLEBADWOLFCHICAGO.COM

6. Brunch so hard at **M.HENRY**, 5707 N. CLARK ST., CHICAGO, (773) 561-1600, MHENRY.NET

7. Spice it up at **MANGO PICKLE**, 5842 N. BROADWAY, CHICAGO, (773) 944-5555, MANGOPICKLECHICAGO.COM

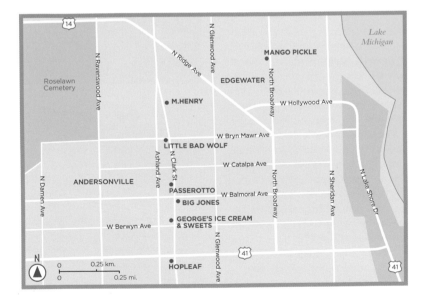

Andersonville & Edgewater

Colorful Food Personality

EDGEWATER IS A LAKEFRONT COMMUNITY about 7 miles north of the Loop and just south of Loyola University. Known for Edgewater and Foster Beaches, it is on the northern border of massive Lincoln Park and Lake Shore Drive. Edgewater was farmland until John Lewis Cochran built the first subdivision in the 1880s and gave the area its name. Once a wealthy "suburb" of Chicago, it continues to be very residential today. Andersonville, a popular neighborhood within Edgewater, is farther inland and has European roots, especially from Sweden. The Swedish American Museum is on Clark Street, Andersonville's main corridor.

Andersonville has a colorful personality with mostly locally owned small businesses and one of the most vibrant LGBT communities in Chicago. Clark Street comes alive on the weekends, and the streets fill with people shopping, eating, and sipping coffee. Andersonville has become one of the most popular neighborhoods on Chicago's North Side and has a very diverse offering of restaurants, bars, bakeries, boutiques, antiques shops, and more. Their summer farmers' market happens every Wednesday and closes down Berwyn Street between Clark and Ashland. Clark and the surrounding streets have great energy and are very pedestrian- and dog-friendly. Take a walk, and you'll see what I mean.

1

HOPLEAF

Owner Michael Roper opened **HOPLEAF** back in 1992, when the neighborhood was sleepy without much going on. He took over an old, run-down liquor store/taproom and transformed it into what Hopleaf is today, a hopping craft-beer-focused bar with a Belgian-inspired, chef-crafted menu. Remaining open for over 25 years is quite impressive, especially in a high-risk industry.

The draft beer menu is expansive and constantly rotating, with a focus on Belgian beers, including the Tripel Karmeliet, a 300-plus-year-old recipe using three kinds of grain: barley, wheat, and oats. They also feature local beers, wine on tap, and draft ciders. With good beer comes good food, and you can't go to Hopleaf without trying their mussels. There are always mussels on the menu prepared two ways, one Belgian-style and one that changes periodically, and you can order for one or two people. The Belgian-style is steamed in Blanche de Chambly and flavored with sliced shallots, celery, thyme, and bay leaves. Sop up the savory broth with the bread and heaping pile of *frites* that it's served with. A palatable charcuterie board is essential to pair with beer, and Hopleaf has a wonderful selection: Chicken liver mousse garnished with jam made with La Fin du Monde, shallots, and currant; pork belly rillettes with dabs of mixed berry jam; summer sausage, spicy smoked duck breast, and head cheese come accompanied by pickled quail eggs and turnips. Spread the grainy mustard on top of a slice of toasted

bread, which goes deliciously well with the cured meat. You can't go wrong with the Steak Frites, a wood-grilled, grass-fed New York strip topped with a dollop of herb butter served with hand-cut *pommes frites* fried in 100 percent canola oil. The Goat Cheese Cheesecake is a great ending to your meal, with a cashew–pine nut–thyme crust, apricot–golden raisin–cherry chutney, and micro arugula. All the ingredients used on the menu are thoughtfully sourced from local farms.

TIP

Grab a gourmet sandwich from their lunch menu, like the Toasted Nueske Ham Sandwich with gruyère and apple-tarragon slaw nestled between toasted pumpernickel bread.

2 GEORGE'S ICE CREAM & SWEETS

GEORGE'S ICE CREAM & SWEETS is an Andersonville staple for all your sugar cravings. Sisters-in-law Anna and Angie Stotis opened the ice cream shop in 2009, inspired by and named after their father/father-in-law, George Stotis. He owned Chicago Recycle Shop, a vintage furniture and clothing store, in the neighborhood for 30 years and loved connecting with people through conversation. He always dreamt about opening a cafe or restaurant in the area where he could bring people together, and so the two women decided to open George's Ice Cream & Sweets to honor his dream. They aspire to be a place for get-togethers, celebrations, and social events where everyone can enjoy quality time with the important people in their lives.

It is always bustling in the shop, especially during the summer. You will find lines out the door if it gets even remotely warm in Chicago. If that is not a sure sign you should enter the doors, I don't know what is. They serve Chocolate Shoppe Ice Cream, all-natural mixes of premium ice cream from Madison, Wisconsin. The flavors rotate, with 32 available daily, like Brownie Cascade, Cake Batter, Espresso Oreo, Salted Caramel, and Yippie Skippee. Both kids and adults go crazy over the colorful Superman ice cream, so why not get three scoops? The sundaes come with two generous scoops of ice cream and are topped with whipped cream, nuts, and a cherry. Try one of their signature sundaes, like the Turtle Sundae with vanilla ice cream, hot fudge, caramel, and pecans, or create your own. Add any of their baked goods (how about a large Pecan Cookie?) as we did to the Cookie Monster Sundae with cookie dough ice cream, hot fudge, Oreos, and sprinkles.

3 BIG JONES

BIG JONES serves Southern food inspired by traditions and history. The menu is seasonal and items change often. Chef and co-owner Paul Fehribach has a strong philosophy of making items in-house, from the pickles to the breads to the condiments. A prime example of his dedication is the Pickle Tasting, a sampling of the house-made pickles, including okra and peppers, served with pimento cheese and home-baked bread. He adapts old-school ethics and techniques to create his award-winning fried chicken with its delicate, crispy skin that's a result of frying in leaf lard, ham drippings, and clarified butter. You can choose two sides from among items such as ham-fat-fried potatoes, turnip greens, creamy grits, petite rouge peas and rice, and sweet potato hash.

The brunch menu features a fiery version of the fried chicken known as the Sweet and Spicy Chicken topped with pickles and a sunny-side up egg sandwiched between a golden-brown, buttery biscuit.

Fehribach's Crawfish Étouffée includes wild-caught crawfish tails smothered in butter with white wine, lemon, and Worcestershire sauce, and served with a mound of white rice. A special treat for dessert is the Calas, or Creole rice fritters that slaves from rice-growing regions of Africa introduced to Louisiana; they are served on a layer of pastry cream, crushed peanuts, and caramel and topped with confectioners' sugar and chocolate sauce,

4 PASSEROTTO

PASSEROTTO is a traditional Korean restaurant helmed by chef-owner Jennifer Kim. The menu is inspired by her Korean heritage with some influences from Italian cuisine. The restaurant's name means "little sparrow" in Italian, a translation of the Korean nickname "chamsae" given to Kim as a child by her father. It also represents her experiences of working in Italian kitchens as well as her travels to Italy. Don't mistake her food as the dreadful word *fusion*! Passerotto is 100 percent Korean. She honors Korean food in her own authentic way as a Korean American and pushes the boundaries with her love for Italian food to bridge the gap between the cultures.

The first section of the menu titled Raw, or *Hwe* in Korean, is reminiscent of some of the revered dishes at the now-closed Snaggletooth, a laid-back counter-service spot Kim once co-owned. The plump, fresh bay scallops are luxuriously plated with splashes of house-made XO sauce, robust soy onion puree, and a citron zing. The thin, crispy *farinata* (a Italian chickpea pancake) with kimchi, charred scallion, and baby garlic pesto is a true testament to the spring season with pops of vibrant green. There is nothing more comforting than a hot bowl of Korean soup, and the Cacciucco Soondubu is exactly that . . . pure comfort. From a quick glance, it looks like *cacciucco*, a Tuscan-style seafood stew with generous pieces of clams, mussels, and prawns. But at first sip, it quickly brings me back to Korean *soondubu* with the slightly sour kimchi broth, silken tofu, and traditional side dishes also known as *banchan*. As in Korean culture and food, sharing is always encouraged.

5 LITTLE BAD WOLF

Don't let the name scare you away. There's nothing "bad" about **LITTLE BAD WOLF** unless you mean b-b-b-b-bad to the bone. This neighborhood gem is enchanting, with Little Red Riding Hood vibes and an extensive list of craft beers and artisanal cocktails. The upscale bar food is notable, with ridiculously good burgers that will make you howl with excitement.

All the cocktails are handcrafted to order using homemade ingredients and fresh juices. Quench your thirst with the Greens Eyes, invigorating matcha green tea infused Tito's, lime, and celery bitters. The El Chupacabra has a tropical feel with the Caña Brava rum, Velvet Falernum, Little Bad Wolf pineapple shrub, lime, and a bit of heat from the Scrappy's Firewater bitters. The food menu is broken out by Pinch, Fold, Grab, and Stab. Pinch your fingers around a flavorful mussel cooked in an intense green coconut curry broth, infused with Allagash white, and sweetened with Asian pear. Grab one of their colossal burgers stacked with three patties, American cheese, onion straws, house-made pickles, and a fried egg. You'll want to take a picture of this one before you devour it. While we are on the gluttonous path, stab your fork right into the Half Fried Chicken served with buttery mashed potatoes and smothered in bacon gravy. The creamy Mac and Cheese with honey-cured bacon, scallions, and toasted bread crumbs is a winner. And whoever thought of topping the *elotes* (Mexican grilled corn) with beer-battered avocados is a genius.

6

M.HENRY

Good things come to those who brunch, and there are a lot of good things going on at **M.HENRY**. This respectable restaurant has been in the neighborhood for over 15 years and still continues to be a well-liked spot for all your brunching needs. It gets crowded, especially on the weekends, so come prepared to wait. Reservations are taken only for parties of eight or more.

The menu features fresh new takes on old-time favorites using clean, natural, and simple ingredients. For sweet options, the Blackberry Bliss Cakes are blissful. Two fluffy pancakes are layered with warm blackberries and vanilla mascarpone, and topped with brown sugar and oat crust. Three slices of brioche french toast stacked with house-made lemon curd and raspberry coulis create the dreamy Lemon-Raspberry Brioche French Toast. For a savory option, Fannie's Killer Fried Egg Sandwich is a classic: A blanket of Gorgonzola cheese covers the bottom of a piece of toasted *boule* bread, topped with applewood-smoked bacon and two over-medium eggs, finished with fresh thyme, and served with a side of house potatoes. Fresh salads are available during lunch, except on Sunday. The Cornucopia Salad is a medley of crisp apples, sweet corn, grape tomatoes, cucumbers, beets, mango, butternut squash, fresh basil, and red onions tossed in a lime balsamic vinaigrette; grilled chicken or salmon are available on the side for an additional charge.

There are several vegan and vegetarian options available, including the Veritable Vegan Epiphany, scrambled organic tofu sautéed with rapini, sweet onions, and house-blend spices. It also comes with a side of veggie sausage and house potatoes.

7 MANGO PICKLE

The smells of Indian spices fill the air as you walk into **MANGO PICKLE**. The space is cozy and inviting with multicolored fabric walls, brightly hued decorative pillows, vivid hanging lights, and ornate art pieces. Chef and co-owner Marisa Paolillo is a Chicago native who lived and traveled throughout India for almost a decade. It was during her time in Mumbai, India, that she decided to make a career change and become a chef. Paolillo worked in various kitchens in India, Italy, and Chicago before deciding to open Mango Pickle with her husband, Nakul Patel, in Edgewater. The menu expresses her interpretation of traditional Indian food, based on her travels and personal experiences, with a modern flair.

The menu is updated daily based on the seasonal ingredients, so whatever you see on today's menu, you may not see tomorrow. The Mung Dal Chila is a savory crepe plated with cilantro-peanut chutney and zesty lemon pickle. The consistency of the crepe holds the flavorsome chutney well with each and every bite. Vegetarian dishes are considerable here, with more than half of the menu dedicated to them. The Spring Green Paneer highlights the current season's best, for example, a medley of summer squash, broccoli, and cauliflower atop a kale purée with green chutney. The Cauliflower "Filet" and Potatoes was incredibly "meaty," with contrasting textures from the whole head of cauliflower, thick-cut potatoes, and toasted almonds. I like anything tikka masala, but not in vegetable form, but spiced with tikka masala and cumin, this dish is bold and gives the routinely uninspired vegetable a flavor boost. The Mahi Mahi Paturi is my favorite item on the menu, as the fish came out perfectly cooked in a banana leaf. Unwrap to reveal the aromas of the mustard seeds and turmeric. The Lamb Biryani is a glorious puff pastry–like dish with seasonal vegetables, cardamom leaf, and fluffy saffron rice, all encompassed by soft naan.

THE EVANSTON CRAWL

1. Pig out at **PECKISH PIG,** 623 HOWARD ST., EVANSTON, (847) 491-6778, THEPECKISHPIG.COM

2. Get bready at **HEWN,** 810 DEMPSTER ST., EVANSTON, (847) 869-4396, HEWNBREAD.COM

3. Sweeten up at **PATISSERIE CORALIE,** 600 DAVIS ST., EVANSTON, (847) 905-0491, BESTFRENCHPASTRIES.COM

4. Sun's out, bun's out at **EDZO'S BURGER SHOP,** 1571 SHERMAN AVE., EVANSTON, (847) 864-3396, EDZOS.COM

5. Dine farm-to-table at **BOLTWOOD,** 804 DAVIS ST., EVANSTON, (847) 859-2880, BOLTWOODEVANSTON.COM

6. Feast your eyes at **NAKORN,** 1622 ORRINGTON AVE., EVANSTON, (847) 733-8424, NAKORNKITCHEN.COM

7. Don't worry, be hoppy at **SMYLIE BROTHERS BREWING COMPANY,** 1615 OAK AVE., EVANSTON, (224) 999-7320, SMYLIEBROS.COM

8. Get the meat sweats at **THE BARN,** 1016 CHURCH ST., EVANSTON, (847) 868-8041, THEBARNEVANSTON.COM

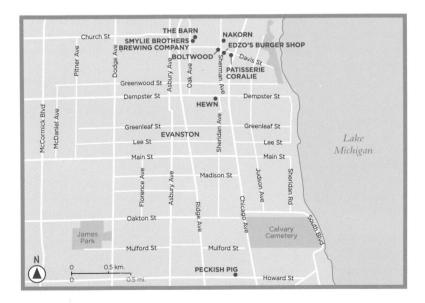

Evanston

Dining Capital of Chicago's North Shore

EVANSTON IS A POPULAR AND TRENDY SUBURB in Chicago's North Shore and my favorite in Chicagoland. Located along the shores of Lake Michigan and only 12 miles north of the Loop, with easy access to public transportation, Evanston is a coveted suburb for professionals of all ages. Also home to Northwestern University, Evanston's lively downtown, which is connected to campus, has a wide range of businesses that cater to the diverse demographic range. Students and residents alike enjoy a nice mix of national chains and independent businesses.

Downtown is centered around the Davis Street Metra and "L" stations, which is a common theme for the rest of Evanston's shopping areas. Commercial districts are close to the Central Street, Dempster, Howard, and Main Street train stations, and are connected by Chicago Avenue, which cuts across each of them. Known as the dining capital of Chicago's North Shore, Evanston has a little bit of everything, including Chicago classics, ethnic foods, steakhouses, bar after bar after bar, and new and trendy cuisines. I've personally done a lot of food crawling around Evanston, and I know you will not be disappointed.

1 PECKISH PIG

Feeling peckish? *Peckish* is a British term meaning "hungry," and it's exactly how you will feel after reading this description. **PECKISH PIG** is a family-owned gastropub located on historic Howard Street in Evanston near Rogers Park. They brew their own beers on-site, which are complemented by an eclectic food menu from owner and executive chef Debbie Evans. Evans has lived in the community with her family for over two decades, and they are also involved in the business. India (daughter) handles the front of house as well as events, while Janek (son) manages the bar. Debbie Evans is originally from Liverpool, England, and before she settled in Evanston, she was a professional dancer who lived in Spain, Japan, and elsewhere, and she fell in love with food. The all-around menu draws upon her travels while still remaining true to her roots.

I say the best way to tackle the menu is order a couple items from each section and share. In the Small Plates section, there are tacos, wings, avocado hummus, and bacon-wrapped dates. I tried the Poke Bowl, a rainbow in a bowl with an abundance of sliced salmon, mango, avocado, cucumber, red onion, and edamame. The flatbreads rotate based on the season, and the roasted peach with goat cheese and baby kale screamed summer. Pasta dishes, fish-and-chips, meats, and steak are featured on the Big Plates section, including Mediterranean Lamb Kebabs served with basmati rice, pickled onion, and parsley. Pork it up with some Slow Roasted Pork Belly with gravy and Kerrygold mashed potatoes. Sandwiches and burgers are also available, like the Beef & Chorizo Burger with port onions and cheese that is served with thick-cut fries. The best way to get your daily fruit intake is on top of the Almond & Coriander Pound Cake, right? I will take it in alcohol form, too. The cocktails are a delight, and the names cheeky. Aloe There is tequila drink with Chareau Aloe Liqueur, lime, celery bitters, cucumber, and a little Tajín spice, while the Early Hours is a gin drink with fruit undertones.

Check out their cool patio during warmer months! Grab one of their house-made brews, like the Gin & Juice IPA with grape-fruit and juniper flavors, or the Strawburied Alive with a sweet strawberry aroma and a slightly sour taste.

2 HEWN

HEWN specializes in hand-forged artisan bread, all naturally fermented with locally sourced organic flours and grains. Until around the 1960s, a few different groceries and bakeries occupied this space, but they soon became extinct. Co-owners Ellen King and Julie Matthei wanted to bring back to Evanston the heart and warmth of those small, family-owned businesses, and they do just that here with pureness and authenticity. This mission reflects not only in what they produce but also in all aspects of the bakery, including the interior furnishings that are made with salvaged and repurposed materials.

The bread selection rotates daily and is made fresh every day. King, who is also the head of the baking operations, explains the process: The dough is mixed and shaped by hand and placed in wicker rising baskets called *bannetons*, where it rises overnight naturally. No two breads are alike, because each takes on different characteristics based on the person who makes it. You can get Marquis Wheat (rare), Cheddar Country (2-year aged white cheddar), and Turkey Red (hearty and earthy) to name a few. The Country Bread, which has been fermented for 17 hours, is baked and available every day. Due to the long fermentation, people with gluten sensitivity can usually enjoy the breads.

While you are there, pick up a few pastries. They come in all shapes and sizes, filled with fruit (strawberry rhubarb galettes), specked with olives (olive brioche), crusted with caramelized sugar (kouign amann), topped with sugar (morning bun), and baked with butter (croissant). It also comes layered with fruit and nuts (bostock) and dripped with glaze (cinnamon brioche).

3

PATISSERIE CORALIE

Swanky chandeliers drape from the ceilings while Parisian-themed art lines the walls. The smell of butter and coffee and the sight of French pastries intensify my hunger, which is somehow smoothed by "La Vie en Rose" playing in the background. Where am I? It doesn't feel like Chicago or Evanston. Owner Pascal Berthoumieux is a French-born restaurateur who is dedicated to bringing French culture to Evanston, and **PATISSERIE CORALIE** does just that. The ambience is charming and quaint, a perfect place for conversations over coffee and bites.

They specialize in freshly baked *viennoiseries* and traditional French pastries, including a wide selection of macarons. All the pastries and treats are handcrafted and made fresh daily. Your infatuation for Patisserie Coralie will start with a kiss. Paris on My Lips, the lip-shaped cake sprayed with red candy, is adorable and seductive. A zesty lime cake is nestled by a mint and lime-zest cream and sits atop a sweet base made with almond coconut cookies. The delicately hued macarons come with creamy fillings in unique flavors like black currant, lychee, rose, Meyer lemon, matcha, blackberry, French lavender, strawberry basil, coconut milk chocolate, and more, and they can be bought individually or in a box of 6 or 12. The Strawberry Shortcake Macaronade is a coupling of an American strawberry shortcake with a French macaron: A giant macaron shell pads the piped Madagascar vanilla bean ganache with a layer of strawberry coulis and fresh strawberries. Creamy lemon curd is enclosed by an almond tart crust and topped with flawless torched meringue on the lemon tart. Phenomenal complements to your morning tea or coffee are the flaky croissants—butter, chocolate, almond, chocolate almond, and apple cinnamon—or the cinnamon raisin roll with golden raisins and almond cream.

4 EDZO'S BURGER SHOP

For the love of burgers, go to **EDZO'S BURGER SHOP** ASAP. Chef-owner Eddie Lakin opened Edzo's, a counter-service burger joint, near the Northwestern campus in 2009, motivated by creating a job to support his family and inspired by the restaurants his father used to take him to as a child.

Lakin takes an upscale approach and applies it to a basic hot dog shop, resulting in a formula that works really well. Organic, locally sourced ingredients are used, and the beef for the burgers is ground and made fresh daily. Massiveness on a bun best describes the 8-ounce Char Burger, a juicy, meaty patty. The 4-ounce Griddled Burger can be stacked with a double or triple patty and topped with ketchup, mustard, and pickle. Enhance your burger with an add-on, like bacon, cheese, a fried egg, jalapeño peppers, and more. Edzo's Burger Shop is not only about the burgers. Lakin plays homage to Chicago foods like the classic Chi-town hot dog (no ketchup!) and the Maxwell Street Polish with grilled onions and mustard. After all the consumption, you may want to exercise. I mean, you should have extra fries. *Yassss to fries!* Their fries are hand-cut throughout the day with a variety of toppings to choose from; Merkts cheddar makes everything better, as in the Cheese Fries. The Buffalo Fries are tossed with buffalo sauce and blue cheese and served with celery sticks. Wash all of it down with an old-fashioned milkshake made with slow-churned ice cream. It'll bring back fond childhood memories.

5 BOLTWOOD

Chef-owner Brian Huston grew up in Evanston, and **BOLT-WOOD** fulfills his life-long goal of opening a restaurant in his hometown, where friends and family are the center, with chef-driven, locally sourced food and generous hospitality. Huston and his wife, Chrissy Prieto, have been serving the Evanston community with warms hearts since 2014.

Huston helped revolutionize farm-to-table cooking during his six years with Paul Kahan at The Publican. The menu changes daily and is driven by the market and seasons, ensuring taste and quality. It's worth filling up on Boltwood's bread. Paired with butter and sea salt, the freshly baked, soft bread is a game changer, and it's great with elegant seasonal soups. Edible flowers float atop the Chilled English Pea Soup, the soup du jour. Huston points out that the Crispy Potatoes are a crowd favorite, and I can see why. A bowl of joy arrives with an abundance of golden-brown potato wedges crisp on the outside with a warm, tender center. When you dip into the garlic schmaltz, aka rendered fat, you get a rich, buttery bite.

The Grilled Peach Salad is a bright compilation topped with a tangy vinaigrette. Share the stunning Roasted Millers Half Chicken topped with pistachio pesto, as the dish is big enough for two. My favorite dish of the night was the Crispy Phoenix Tofu served with coconut rice. It had a spicy finish that balanced well with the pickled onions. Everyone passing by was pointing at the cheesecake with macerated blueberries and asking, "What is that? Looks so good." In this case, pointing in public is acceptable and encouraged.

NAKORN

Business partners and co-founders Sam Rattanopas and Mina Sudsaard grew up together in Bangkok, Thailand, and have been best friends since the third grade. They left everything behind and immigrated together to the United States in 1996, when they were in their 20s. Longing for the tastes of their native country, they opened **NAKORN** to re-create some of their families' recipes and bring a little bit of home to the States. They wanted to share the authentic flavors from their childhood with the neighborhood of Evanston. Old-world recipes with modern presentation in a homey atmosphere make for an enjoyable meal out for any occasion.

NaKorn means "metropolitan" in Thai and has three significances to the restaurant.

1. Bangkok is the largest metropolitan city in Thailand.

2. It's representative of their urban approach to traditional dishes.

3. Rattanopas's father, Khun Sompit Rattanopas, is from the city of Nakhon Si Thammarat, and the restaurant was named NaKorn to honor him.

The seasonal dinner menu is categorized by Bites, Green, Meat, and Sea. In the Bites section, the Crab Cake Bites is one of the most popular items, and understandably so. A blend of crabmeat, pork, taro, and water chestnuts is rolled in soy paper, fried into a light crisp, and topped with a fresh cucumber and a hunk of crab meat. It is garnished with beet-infused lotus root, sliced plum, spring greens, and house-made plum gastrique. The rice and noodle dishes are absolutely stunning and worth writing home about. I couldn't get over the gorgeous Butterfly Pea Flower Rice and Thai Herbs, a mound of naturally dyed blue rice surrounded by an assortment of seasonal vegetables and pomelo served with a house-made vegetarian *naam budu* sauce. Celebrate life with the Bangkok Chinatown Stir-Fried Longevity Noodles served on a bed of sautéed green cabbage, spring carrots, shiitake mushrooms, and other seasonal ingredients. Other standouts are the Kobocha-Kale Chicken Roulade with the bold flavors of the kabocha–Thai chile curry sauce, or the Rainbow Trout dressed with a lemongrass-tamarind-coconut reduction and brightened with watermelon radishes, English cucumbers, fried shallots, and pomegranate seeds. NaKorn is a full-service restaurant with a splendid drinks list. Cool down with a Bangkok Mule, mixed with house-made kaffir lime–infused vodka,

and the Windmill Ginger Brew, served in a silver Thai drinking cup. Details on the desserts are impressive as well. I could eat a few plates of the Fresh Mango, Coconut-Sweet Sticky Rice with a sweet and tangy mango sorbet, salted coconut sauce, and toasted coconut flakes. The liquid mango yolk is like a flavor explosion in your mouth.

7 SMYLIE BROTHERS BREWING COMPANY

Family, brews, and barbecue are at the center of **SMYLIE BROTHERS BREWING COMPANY.** With his love for beer and Texas barbecue (their dad was from San Antonio), Michael Smylie and his four brothers opened Smylie Brothers Brewing Company in 2014.

If you like drinking beer on the days ending in the letter *y*, this is your place. Beers that are available year-round, as well as seasonal and specialty beers, are brewed on-site. The House Lager is always on the menu, a Bavarian-style pale lager with a crisp, clean flavor highlighting pilsner malt and lightly hopped with noble hops from Germany. A customer-favorite seasonal beer is the Pride of Clement, an Extra Special/Strong Bitter (ESB) brewed using traditional British ingredients with a moderate hop bitterness. Tasters, drafts, growlers, and growler refills are available for your enjoyment.

A great mix of Midwestern comfort food and Texas-style barbecue is showcased on the menu with the brisket as the star; it is simply seasoned and slow smoked over oak and applewood for about 14 hours. The Company Burger is a mouthful with two 4-ounce griddled Angus beef patties packed with all the fixings in a potato bun. And, since pizza and beers go hand and hand, they offer an assortment of wood-fired pizzas. Remember that brisket? Yep, you can get it on a pizza as well. The Spinach & Marinated Mushroom Pizza was straightforward but satisfying. Fill your belly with pork belly, as in the Pork Belly Poutine with house-cut fries, beer-braised pork belly, Wisconsin cheese curds, California Common gravy, and Kansas City barbecue sauce. Add a fried egg or bacon for an additional cost.

8 THE BARN

THE BARN is a farm-chic, meat-focused restaurant restored from what used to be a horse barn for the Borden Condensed Milk Company back in the 1880s. You may get a little lost finding it, as it is tucked down an alleyway between Oak and Maple Avenues. A shimmering chandelier dangles in the main dining room, while the portrait of an alpaca named George is a focal point on the wall.

The Barn, proprietor Amy Morton's second restaurant in Evanston, is a nod to Morton's The Steakhouse, a classic steakhouse her father, Arnie Morton, established. The Escolar Ceviche with lime juice, cucumber, avocado, and oranges is citrusy and zesty, with a little spice from jalapeño. Caviar dreams are possible when you order the luxurious Grand Central Caviar Sandwich. Wild American bowfin caviar with a farm egg and crème fraîche is packed between two slices of soft bread. A cart is wheeled up to your table as the Little Gem and Creamy Dijon Salad is prepared tableside, with an option to add bacon and/ or anchovies. A wonderful fish option is the delightful seared halibut served with an herb puree and a medley of asparagus, mushrooms, and spinach. You can chose from several steaks, including a bone-in rib eye, filet mignon, center strip Manhattan cut, but the beefy Tomahawk served with marrow–German Butterball potatoes is just plain jaw-dropping. Pour on the red wine demiglace for extra flavor. Meat sweats, no regrets.

Bonus Crawls!

Chicago Favorites

From Chicago-style hot dogs to Italian beef sandwiches and deep-dish pizzas, here are a few must-stops for Chicago favorite dishes.

THE CHICAGO FAVORITES CRAWL

1. **THE ORIGINAL MAXWELL STREET**, 601 S. SACRAMENTO BLVD., CHICAGO, (773) 722-7360, THEORIGINALMAXWELLSTREET.COM

2. **GARRETT POPCORN SHOPS** (MULTIPLE LOCATIONS), 4 E. MADISON ST., CHICAGO, (888) 476-7267, GARRETTPOPCORN.COM

3. **JOHNNIE'S BEEF** (TWO LOCATIONS), 7500 W. NORTH AVE., ELMWOOD PARK, (708) 452-6000

4. **PORTILLO'S HOT DOGS** (MULTIPLE LOCATIONS), 100 W. ONTARIO, CHICAGO, (312) 587-8910, PORTILLOS.COM

5. **GENE & JUDE'S**, 2720 N. RIVER RD., RIVER GROVE, (708) 452-7634, GENEANDJUDES.COM

6. **LOU MALNATI'S PIZZERIA** (MULTIPLE LOCATIONS), 6649 LINCOLN AVE., LINCOLNWOOD, LOUMALNATIS.COM

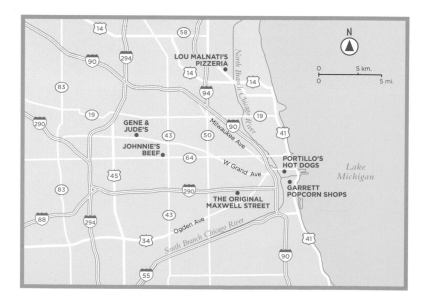

1 THE ORIGINAL MAXWELL STREET

Follow the big yellow sign to **THE ORIGINAL MAXWELL STREET** walk-up window and put in your order. The chunky Maxwell Street Polish comes nuzzled in

a bun slathered with mustard and peppers and blanketed with copious amounts of caramelized onions. All sandwiches come with fries, but get an upgrade with the Maxwell Steak Cheese Fries doused with melty cheese and chunks of steak. Open 24 hours, it is cash only.

2 GARRETT POPCORN SHOPS

Since 1949, there has been no one *butter* than **GARRETT POPCORN SHOPS** for some handcrafted gourmet popcorn. Every bag and tin is made on-site in small batches. The kernels

are hot-air-popped and mixed with the secret Chody family ingredients in old-school copper kettles. The true Chicagoan order is the Garrett Mix, a sweet-and-salty blend of their signature CaramelCrisp and CheeseCorn recipes. Expect sticky caramel teeth, yellow cheddar fingers, and a happy, satisfied tummy. The year-round menu also includes Plain, Buttery, and a few other CaramelCrisp versions. Love you bucket loads, Garrett Popcorn Shops!

3

JOHNNIE'S BEEF

Since 1961, **JOHNNIE'S BEEF** has been a legendary spot for a classic Italian beef sandwich. The lines

are long at this cash-only eatery, but the service is quick. The menu is straightforward with Italian beef, Italian sausage, combo (sausage and beef), Italian ice, and more. The most popular item is the Italian beef, thinly sliced, garlicky beef stuffed into chewy, Italian bread with your choice of sweet (bell peppers), hot peppers (giardiniera), or both. I like mine with both, and I get it "juicy," meaning they dip the sandwich into the savory, spice-filled jus, aka "gravy," creating a hot mess, but that is all part of the Johnnie's experience. The Italian sausage has a nice snap and can also be ordered with your preferred pepper offerings. Pair it with the legendary, house-made Italian ice, which comes in only one flavor—lemon. Cash only, and seats are limited to a few picnic tables outside.

4

PORTILLO'S HOT DOGS

Founder Dick Portillo opened The Dog House, Portillo's first hot dog stand, in 1963 in Villa Park. Portillo invested $1,100 to start his business, and now it's worth billions, with over 50 chain locations nationwide. Whether you live in Chicago or you are visiting, there's no denying people love their **PORTILLO'S**. It can be a little overwhelming at first, with neon signs, loud screaming over the intercom, and crowds of people looking for seats, but take a deep breath; everything will

be OK. Get in line, put your order in at the counter, and wait for your number to be called. My usual go-to consists of Italian beef with hot peppers, a Chicago-style hot dog with everything, chopped salad, cheese fries, and their famous chocolate cake. Let the eating begin!

GENE & JUDE'S

In 1945, Gene Mormino felt there was something missing from the hot dogs at Wrigley Field and began experimenting. Mormino and friend Jude DeSantis brought **GENE & JUDE'S** to River Grove in 1950, and they have been serving the neighborhood since. There are only three choices on the menu: hot dog, double dog, and corn tamale. The hot dogs are a home run with mustard, relish, onions, sport peppers, and fries stacked high.

> "No seats. No ketchup. No pretense. No nonsense."
>
> —*Gene & Jude's*

LOU MALNATI'S PIZZERIA

Nothing says Chicago food like deep-dish pizza, and **LOU MALNATI'S** is a Chicago favorite among many. Lou Malnati and his wife, Jean, opened their first location in Lincolnwood in 1971. After the passing of Lou in 1978, his sons Marc and Rick joined the business, and they still lead the enterprise today. They are committed to quality and use only exceptional ingredients. Their tomatoes are grown in California, and each year they go to personally meet the tomato growers. The cheese comes from a dairy farm in Wisconsin, the same supplier they have been using for over 40 years. The flaky, buttery crust is a secret family recipe that was passed down from Grandpa Malnati in the 1940s. The Deep Dish Malnati Chicago Classic (lean sausage, mozzarella cheese, and vine-ripened tomato sauce) and Deep Dish Pepperoni are always a sure win. If you must go thin, the thin crust The Lou, with a mix of spinach, garlic, basil, onion, mushrooms, sliced Roma tomatoes, and three cheeses, will be a hit.

Hottest Doughnuts in Town

I *doughnut* want to work out. I'm on a D.I.E.T. (Did I eat that?) Here are the top spots in Chicago for doughnuts.

THE DOUGHNUT CRAWL

1. **THE DAPPER DOUGHNUT**, 131 N. CLINTON ST., CHICAGO, (773) 392-1300, THEDAPPERDOUGHNUT.COM

2. **FIRECAKES** (MULTIPLE LOCATIONS), 68 W. HUBBARD ST., CHICAGO, (312) 329-6500, FIRECAKESDONUTS.COM

3. **DO-RITE DONUTS** (MULTIPLE LOCATIONS), 50 W. RANDOLPH ST., CHICAGO, (312) 488-2483, DORITEDONUTS.COM

4. **STAN'S DONUTS & COFFEE** (MULTIPLE LOCATIONS), 1560 N. DAMEN AVE., CHICAGO, (773) 360-7386, STANSDONUTSCHICAGO.COM

5. **UPTOWN DONUTS**, 1122 W. WILSON AVE., CHICAGO, (773) 942-6215

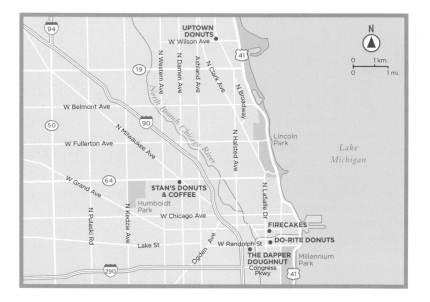

1

THE DAPPER DOUGHNUT

THE DAPPER DOUGH-NUT, formerly Beavers Coffee & Donuts and located inside the Chicago French Market, specializes in made-to-order, mini doughnuts. First, choose your size: mini (4 doughnuts), small (6 doughnuts), medium (12 doughnuts), or large

(24 doughnuts). Then your toppings—there is a variety of flavor combinations to pick from, including the Blueberry Lemon (vanilla sauce, lemon curd, and blueberry), Strawberry Bella (strawberry sauce and graham cracker crumbs), S'mores (chocolate sauce, marshmallow sauce, and graham cracker crumbs), So Krispy (marshmallow and Rice Krispies), and Sweet Stache (honey and chopped pistachios). Good (fried) things come in small packages.

2

FIRECAKES

Jonathan and Karen Fox opened **FIRECAKES,** a small-batch doughnut shop, in honor of Karen's grandfather William "Billy" Hobbs. Hobbs made "firecakes," aka doughnuts, in an oil-filled cast-iron pot over an open fire in the logging camps of northern Wisconsin during the 1930s. His original recipe is the basis of Firecakes Chicago, with some modern touches. You can find classics like the Buttermilk Old Fashioned and

Tahitian Vanilla Iced, alongside rotating seasonal doughnuts, and specialty donuts like Coconut Cream, Maple Glazed Pineapple and Bacon, and Peanut Butter & Jelly. And, because having a plain ice cream sandwich is so basic, try the blissful doughnut ice cream sandwich.

3

DO-RITE DONUTS

Chefs Francis Brennan and Jeff Mahin always dreamt of opening their own doughnut shop, and in 2012, their dreams became a reality with **DO-RITE DONUTS**. The doughnuts are made in small batches utilizing seasonal ingredients. A couple of customer favorites include the Pistachio-Meyer Lemon (cake doughnut with Meyer lemon glaze and coated with Sicilian pistachios) and Candied Maple Bacon (classic yeast-raised doughnut dipped in maple glaze and topped with pieces of candied bacon). You may also find Michigan Apple Fritters dipped in cinnamon glaze, an Old Fashioned rolled in cinnamon sugar, or Valrhona Chocolate Cake doughnut swirled with chocolate ganache. The rotating flavors change frequently based on what the chefs want to create, but whatever you're in the mood for, you will want to go early. They close once they are sold out, and you *do not* want to miss out! Vegan and gluten-free choices are also available, as well as the option to swap out the brioche bun on any of their sandwiches for a doughnut. Can I say doughnut chicken sandwich? *Stahhhp!*

4

STAN'S DONUTS & COFFEE

STAN'S DONUTS & COFFEE in Chicago is a partnership between Stan Berman (founder of the legendary Stan's Donuts in LA) and Rich Labriola (founder of Labriola Baking Company). Bonded by their passion for baking, the duo were inspired to bring Berman's famous doughnuts to Chicago, and Stan's Donuts & Coffee in Chicago was born. The decor is adorable with splashes of pink and a wall full of colorful Kitchen Aid mixers. Labriola uses his recipes to put spins on Stan's classics. The doughnuts are fried fresh every day and include

everything from glazed, sprinkled, and powdered to stuffed, twisted, and rolled.

5

UPTOWN DONUTS

Partners Thi Kim and Sal Bahad opened **UPTOWN DONUTS** in their home neighborhood in 2018. Donuts are handcrafted and include glazed, frosted, cakes/buttermilks, and specialty doughnuts. Cakes/buttermilks come frosted with fruity flavors like blueberry, cherry, orange, and strawberry, as well as specialty flavors like matcha, ube (purple yam), maple, and cinna-glaze. Chicagoans love to top everything with cereal, so it is no surprise the doughnuts crested with Fruity Pebbles and Cap'n Crunch are top sellers. The S'mores will have you screaming for s'more.

Best Pizza

Whether you're team deep-dish or thin-crust, Chicago undeniably has some of the best pizza places in the country. Bring your dough, as here are the pizza places you *knead* in your life.

THE PIZZA CRAWL

1. **GIORDANO'S** (MULTIPLE LOCATIONS), 6314 S. CICERO AVE., CHICAGO, (773) 585-6100, GIORDANOS.COM

2. **COALFIRE** (TWO LOCATIONS), 1321 W. GRAND AVE., CHICAGO, (312) 226-2625, COALFIRECHICAGO.COM

3. **SPACCA NAPOLI PIZZERIA**, 1769 W. SUNNYSIDE AVE., CHICAGO, (773) 878-2420, SPACCANAPOLIPIZZERIA.COM

4. **PEQUOD'S PIZZA** (TWO LOCATIONS), 8520 FERNALD AVE., MORTON GROVE, (773) 327-1512, PEQUODSPIZZA.COM

5. **PIECE BREWERY AND PIZZERIA**, 1927 W. NORTH AVE., CHICAGO, (773) 772-4422, PIECECHICAGO.COM

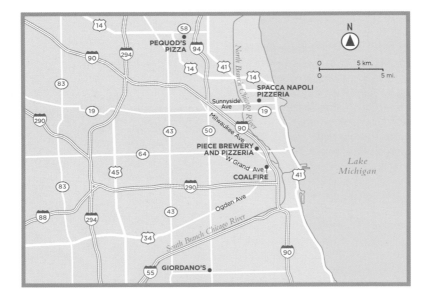

1 GIORDANO'S

GIORDANO'S famous pizza started in Chicago in 1974 and now has expanded to over 50 locations nationwide. The story starts in Torino, Italy, where Mama Giordano was known for her amazing cooking and her Italian Easter Pie. Brothers Efren and Joseph Boglio emigrated from Italy and brought their mom's beloved recipe to Chicago. Thanks to them, we can all enjoy a little piece of pizza-pie heaven! Their super-thick Famous Stuffed Deep Dish comes in different variations of meats, cheeses, and veggies with the option to build your own. Rumor has it they have the cheesiest pull, so I had to test it for myself with the Extra Cheese Deep Dish. I took a shot at my first pull and thought it was pretty impressive. Then I pulled it a little farther and, lo and behold, it went over my head. *Whaaaaaaat?* This has to be a world-record cheese pull. Guinness World Records, call me, a'ight? They also offer hand-stretched thin crust and crispy extra-thin crust if you're not looking to break any records.

2

COALFIRE

At **COALFIRE**, it's all about the thin-crust, coal-fired pizza, and I am super into it. In 2007, partners Dave Bonomi and William Carroll opened their first location in West Town and, in 2015, their second in Lakeview. They wanted to bring a different kind of pizza to Chicago that may not necessarily fall into a certain style of pizza, like Neopolitan or New Haven–style pizza, but is Coalfire style. The pizzas are baked in the 1,500-degree oven that is fueled by clean burning coal, which creates a bubbly, chewy crust with a slight char. You have probably seen the Pepperoni & Whipped Ricotta all over Instagram, with mozzarella, thick-cut pepperoni, ricotta, garlic, and basil. Slice, slice, baby! A few fan favorites are Sopressata & Broccolini with a house-made chile oil and mint, classic Margherita, and Jalapeño with pepperoni and scallions. For something a little distinctive, try the Bacon Jam with mozzarella, sopressata, stracciatella, and chives.

SPACCA NAPOLI PIZZERIA

Pizza is life at **SPACCA NAPOLI**—a way of life. Owners Jon Goldsmith and Ginny Sykes opened in Ravenswood over a decade ago. They are committed to preserving the traditions and energy of Naples, Italy, with thoughtfully crafted food and a family-friendly atmosphere. Goldsmith, a certified *pizzaiuolo* (pizza maker), stays authentic to the Neapolitan-style pizza using trusted Italian producers and an oven built by artisans in Napoli. The dough is tended daily and has a perfectly crispy edge and chewy center. My favorites are the red pizzas with blended San Marzano tomatoes. From a simple Margherita to Funghi e Salsiccia (mushrooms and Italian sausage), you'll want a pizza like this. Provola, prosciutto di Parma, arugula, and Parmigiano Reggiano top the Prosciutto e Rucola. One bite takes me back on my trip to Italy. Food is best enjoyed when it evokes a memory, and Spacca Napoli does just that.

4 PEQUOD'S PIZZA

PEQUOD'S PIZZA specializes in pan (not deep-dish) pizza with a caramelized crust. Yes, caramelized crust. In pizza we *crust*. Traditional deep-dish pizza is baked in a round steel pan with the dough pushed against the top. Instead of dough on the edges, Pequod's Pizza uses cheese, which forms a chewy, burnt crust. The sauce is sweet and tangy and balances all the cheese. This tasty combo has attracted a cult following in both the suburbs (Morton Grove) and the city (Lincoln Park). Customize your pie with any of their fresh toppings, or get it Chicago-style with a premium topping like meatballs or Italian beef. Thin-crust pizzas are available as well as personal size during lunch.

5 PIECE BREWERY AND PIZZERIA

Proprietor Bill Jacobs, a native of New Haven, Connecticut, opened **PIECE BREWERY AND PIZZERIA** with the belief that his hometown had the nation's best pizza. In a city with biased feelings about deep-dish, thick-crust pizza, it was a risky venture to bring an unfamiliar style of pizza to Chicago, but he's made it work. The pizzas are hand-formed and have character. You can get a white pizza with a plain crust brushed with olive oil, diced garlic, and mozzarella cheese, or a red pizza with traditional tomato sauce and mozzarella cheese. The New Haven Style is made with red sauce and topped with garlic and Parmesan instead of mozzarella. My all-time favorite is the Hot Doug's Atomic Sausage Pizza by the legendary Doug Sohn, with his famous Atomic sausage, caramelized onions, and Pepper Jack cheese. Share a New Haven style pie and wash it down with one of their award-winning beers.

Best Sushi

Food is art and art is food. Soo dreams of sushi at these places.

THE SUSHI CRAWL

1. **MOMOTARO,** 820 W. LAKE ST., CHICAGO, (312) 733-4818, MOMOTAROCHICAGO.COM

2. **KATANA,** 339 N. DEARBORN ST., CHICAGO, (312) 877-5544, KATANACHICAGO.COM

3. **KAI ZAN,** 2557 W. CHICAGO AVE., CHICAGO, (773) 278-5776, EATATKAIZAN.COM

4. **NAOKI SUSHI,** 2300 N. LINCOLN PARK WEST, STE. N, CHICAGO, (773) 868-0002, NAOKI-SUSHI.COM

5. **JUNO,** 2638 N. LINCOLN AVE., CHICAGO, (773) 935-2000, JUNOSUSHICHICAGO.COM

6. **RAISU JAPANESE FINE DINING,** 2958 W. IRVING PARK RD., CHICAGO, (773) 961-7299, RAISUSUSHI.COM

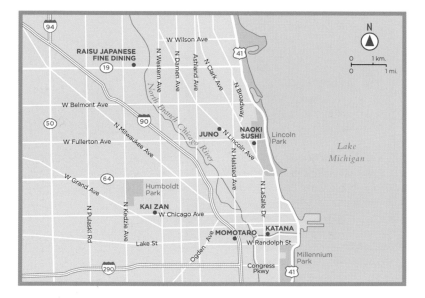

1

MOMOTARO

MOMOTARO is a modern Japanese restaurant with an elegant ambience. The menu changes frequently based on the seasons and availability, but some items remain constant, like the Momomaki, a signature roll with bigeye tuna, spicy tako, and pickled daikon. The Maguro No Namero in the cold section is a cylinder-shaped Balfegó tuna tartare, served with taro chips and wild wasabi. Individual nigiri can be ordered by the piece, like the Hokkaido Hotate (scallop, uni, ikura) or Ika to Sake (spear squid, ikura, smoked salmon). The five-piece Vegetarian Nigiri Selection highlights seasonal vegetables atop sushi rice. If you are a sushi addict like me, go for the Sushi to Sashimi, chef's choice of 5 seasonal nigiri and 8 slices of seasonal sashimi.

2

KATANA

KATANA is a swanky, energetic Japanese restaurant where you want to see and be seen. The fish is fresh and can be prepared in a signature roll, nigiri, or sashimi. Hawaiian kampachi sits in a pool of almond-chile-garlic oil with floating roe. Salmon Sashimi wraps snuggly around the crispy Fuji apples and is garnished with osetra caviar and shaved green onions. The fantastic Sashimi Sampler offers stunning variety, and tuna lovers will rejoice over the Tuna Sampler. Let's roll on over to the next sushi spot in the crawl.

3 KAI ZAN

The **KAI ZAN** menu includes Appetizers, Omakase, Kai Zan Favorites, Charcoal Skewers, Teppan, and Desserts. The seasonal specials, like the Uni Toro Tartare, are incredible. You can't go wrong with anything under the Kai

Zan Favorites. The Orange Rush is a scallop wrapped in salmon and lightly seared with citrus glaze, while the Angry Crab is spicy crab wrapped in fresh tuna and topped with tempura crunch. Soy- and truffle oil–soaked scallions top the Escolar and Maguro Pearls, a tantalizing bite. They have a few rolls, but if you have something in mind, they can make it for you. Reservations are highly recommended.

4 NAOKI SUSHI

NAOKI SUSHI is a Japanese restaurant hidden behind the kitchen of Stratford on the Park in The Belden-Stratford. With a hidden entrance and passageway through the kitchen, it has an underground dining feel to it. The dimly lit, intimate space seats around 50

people, and there's a sushi bar and a few booths for bigger groups. Don't expect anything with cream cheese—tradition and impeccable preparation rule here! You will find Scallop Sashimi with black truffle, yuzu, and soy, or Salmon Sashimi with a kick of spicy ginger soy sauce and pickled red cabbage. The Hamachi Sashimi comes in the shape of a flower, blooming over ponzu and dolloped with *ají panca* (Peruvian red pepper).

5 JUNO

Count on **JUNO** for notable sushi that doesn't completely break the bank. The Signature Smoked Hamachi is a showstopper, its glass dome filled with cedar smoke that permeates the room. Pieces of hamachi rest on a serving spoon with shiitake and sweet corn.

Cold Appetizers include uni shooters, oysters, toro tartare, and the crudo with white fish, ikura, chives, and truffle oil. A few signature and traditional makis are offered with simple ingredients, like the Sake Yaki (grilled salmon sashimi, almond, apple). Watching chef-owner B. K. Park make nigiri is a craft to be appreciated, so order a few and sneak a peek at his skills.

6 RAISU JAPANESE FINE DINING

RAISU JAPANESE FINE DINING specializes in high-quality sushi and sashimi with friendly service in an approachable, relaxed atmosphere. The fish is flown twice a week from Japan and beyond, so it is always served fresh and never frozen. Expect affordable prices and beautiful presentation. Highlights include the sashimi-style Seasonal Whole Fish, and the specially crafted Signature Nigiri. Only the highest grade bluefin tuna is served in the Toro Sashimi. Specialty rolls include the Hi Jack with tempura shrimp, cream cheese, avocado,

scallion, sesame seeds, spicy mayonnaise, unagi sauce, and tempura flakes. Try the *omakase*—let chef Simon Liew customize your meal based on your taste and budget.

Index